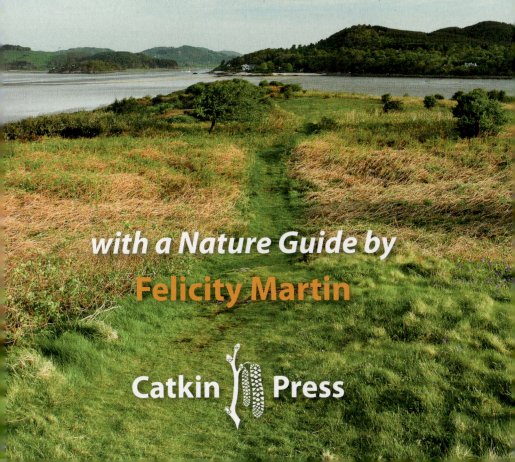

Galloway

25 WALKS

Exploring the Natural Heritage
of Southwest Scotland

Keith Fergus

with a Nature Guide by

Felicity Martin

Catkin Press

First published in Great Britain in 2012 by Catkin Press

Ellangowan, Polinard, Comrie, Perthshire PH6 2HJ
www.catkinpress.com

Copyright © Keith Fergus and Felicity Martin, 2012

Walks guide text and photography: Keith Fergus
Nature guide text, photography, mapping and design: Felicity Martin

The moral rights of the authors have been asserted.

Contains Ordnance Survey data © Crown copyright and database right [2012].

Walk maps are based on Ordnance Survey Mapping reproduced by permission of Ordnance Survey on behalf of HMSO. © Crown copyright 2012. All rights reserved. Ordnance Survey Licence number 100048965

ISBN 978-1-907101-04-5

A CIP catalogue for this book is available from the British Library.

Printed in Scotland by Scotprint
Gateside Commerce Park, Haddington. East Lothian EH41 3ST

Contents

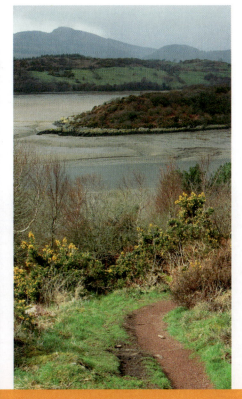

COVER: *The magnificent clifftop walk along the Mull of Galloway (walk 9)*

TITLE PAGE: *Looking across Rough Firth from the summit of Rough Island (walk 4)*

OPPOSITE: *Sunset over Mersehead Sands from Southerness (walk 7) silhouettes Bengairn and Screel*

LEFT: *View over Rough Firth and Glen Isle to Screel from above Kippford (walk 10)*

Introduction

The **Galloway Coast** is very much part of Scotland's windswept western seaboard and has a great deal to offer, particularly to anyone with a fervour for wildlife watching. As the southernmost part of Scotland, it has a less harsh environment than elsewhere on the west coast, because it benefits from the warming influence of the Gulf Stream and is sheltered from the full force of Atlantic storms by the landmass of Ireland to the west.

Hills, lochs, woodland, beaches, rivers and cliffs line the spectacular coastline, providing an enormous variety of habitats for a wide range of plants and animals. Around every corner a new wildlife sight awaits – maybe a carpet of wildflowers or a mighty basking shark.

This guidebook covers the coast of Dumfries and Galloway, which includes the old counties of Dumfriesshire, Kirkcudbrightshire and Wigtownshire. It is a complex coastline, with many bays, headlands and small islands, and totals over 200 miles in length. Starting near Gretna in the east, it runs west along the north shore of the Solway Firth and encompasses the remote landscape of The Machars and the Rhins of Galloway.

The attractive towns and villages along the coast all have their own character, and offer great food, refreshments, shopping and accommodation. Most of the start points for the walks are served by public transport, so a car is not essential to make use of this guidebook.

The 25 walks have been specifically chosen to emphasise the incredible walking opportunities that exist for anyone with a passion for the outdoors: from easy strolls along beaches and through woodland to rough, tough routes along cliff-tops and over hills. They illustrate the Galloway coast's breathtaking scenery, its fascinating history, and the truly exceptional wildlife of this wonderful part of Scotland.

ABOVE: *Rough Firth from the Mote of Mark (walk 10)*

Walking in Galloway

Today most of Dumfries and Galloway remains rural, with agriculture and forestry having played dominant roles over the centuries in its economy and employment. (Agriculture accounts for 70% of the area of the region and woodland a further 25%). Much of the coastline, away from the three biggest towns of Dumfries, Stranraer and Annan, is punctuated by small settlements, rolling pastures with miles of perfectly built dry-stane dykes and pockets of broadleaved woodland.

The climate, influenced by the Gulf Stream, is warm and windy, with plenty of rain thrown in for good measure. It provides suitable conditions for an outstanding array of flora and fauna, much of which can be enjoyed when walking the coastline. Red squirrels, roe deer, great spotted woodpecker, goldcrest and nuthatch thrive in birch, beech, hazel, hawthorn, oak and sycamore woodland, whilst otter, kingfisher and heron are common sights along the riverbanks. Small copper, red admiral and small white butterflies, blue-tailed damselflies and hawker dragonflies flit around the coastline, hedgerows and high moorland along with swift, swallow and skylark.

The countryside is awash with colour through the seasons. Sea pinks and harebell thrive on the grassy clifftops, red campion and tufted vetch grow in the hedgerows, wood anemone and ramsons carpet the woodland, whilst blaeberry, cotton grass and orchids pattern the moorland.

With such a vast coastline you would expect a superb array of birdlife and Galloway really excels: curlew, cormorant, dunlin, greenshank, redshank, knot, barnacle and pink-footed geese, oystercatcher and sandpiper are just a selection to be found on the beaches, estuaries and mudflats, whilst the cliffs are home to the likes of fulmar, shag, puffin and razorbill. Birds of prey include sparrowhawk, peregrine, osprey, buzzard, kestrel and the red kite, which has been reintroduced to the region – with incredible success – over the last decade or so.

As well as this spectacular wildlife, there are breath-taking landscapes and some of the finest panoramas to be found in Britain. The walks provide intimate views of Galloway's coast, rivers, woodland, towns and villages, whilst vantage points such as Cairnsmore of Fleet (walk 25), Criffel (walk 24), Screel (walk 19), Mull of Galloway (walk 9) and The Muckle (walk 10), offer astonishing views to distant Ayrshire, Ireland, Kintyre, the Isle of Man and the magnificent mountains of the Lake District.

Rushing the walks risks missing something along the way. Take time to enjoy the places, wildlife and scenery, all of which combine to make this slice of Scotland's celebrated coastline extraordinary.

BELOW: *Wigtown Bay from Cairnsmore of Fleet (walk 24)*

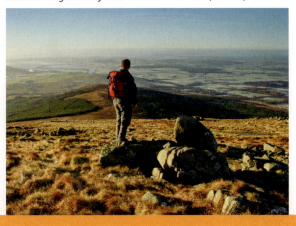

A unique landscape

Dumfries and Galloway is Scotland's third largest region and one of the most sparsely populated areas in Europe; in 2011 it had approximately 148,000 inhabitants with a population density of 60 people per square mile. Compare that to the Scottish average of 168 people per square mile and you will understand why a real sense of space and freedom is experienced when walking in Galloway. There is definitely room to breathe.

The wide, rolling landscapes, with endless grassy pasture, are home to cattle that exemplify Galloway's special character. The native black Galloway and the much-loved Belted Galloway (affectionately known as the Beltie) have evolved to thrive in this distinctive environment.

Both breeds have a coarse outer coat, which helps shed rain, and a soft undercoat providing insulation. The Galloway dates back several hundred years and is one of the oldest and purest of Scotland's cattle breeds, whilst the conspicuous Beltie seems to have arisen from crossbreeding with the Dutch Lakenvelder cattle.

Galloway's history, complexities of language, culture and remoteness from urban Scotland give it a distinct feel, one that is hard to put your finger on – but spend time walking the hills or coastline and it will become clearer. Galloway even has its own anthem, *Bonnie Gallowa'*, and the song's lyrics possibly best sum up the magnificent landscape:

> *Land o' darkly rollin' Dee,*
> *Land o' silvery windin' Cree,*
> *Kissed by Solway's foamy sea,*
> *Bonnie Gallowa'.*

ABOVE: *View over Rockcliffe and Rough Firth to Bengairn and Screel from the Kippford to Sandyhills route (walk 21)*

BELOW: *A Belted Galloway bullock*

Land of the Foreign Gael

The **region's history** extends back many thousands of years with much evidence of Iron Age forts, crannogs and early Christian sites, along with a magnificent array of abbeys and castles, built from the 12th century onwards. With such a lengthy coastline, strong trade links were established with England and Europe, although the ruggedness and extent of the coastline caused its own problems, as smuggling was prevalent for hundreds of years.

The area wasn't called Galloway until the 11th century when it was named after a people, known as the Gall Gaidheil, *the Foreign Gaels*. They were a Norse race from Scandinavia and the Hebrides who dominated the area from the 9th century, replacing rulers from the north of England. Their dominant language was Gaelic, which developed into a distinct dialect called Galwegian (which also drew heavily from Manx and Ulster Irish) but is, sadly, now extinct.

During the Dark Ages the western half of the region was known as the Kingdom of Galloway and it was an independent, Gaelic speaking kingdom. Galloway only became a part of Scotland in 1234. Later, the region was divided into three distinct counties, Wigtownshire and Kirkcudbrightshire to the west and Dumfriesshire to the east.

The two largest towns in the region have their roots in Gaelic: Dumfries (walk 5) translates as *Fortress of the Woodland* and Stranraer as *Place of the Fat Peninsula*. The wonderful hill of Criffel (walk 24), rising above the Solway Firth a few miles from Dumfries, means *Raven Hill* from the Norse Kraka-fjell, the raven being the sacred bird of Scandinavia. The Solway Firth also has Norse origins and translates as *Firth of the Muddy Ford*, whilst The River Dee (walk 3, Gaelic, *Divine River*) and Kirkcudbright (walks 2 and 3, Scots/Old English, *Church of*

St Cuthbert) further illustrate the fascinating historical relationship language has with the Galloway Coast.

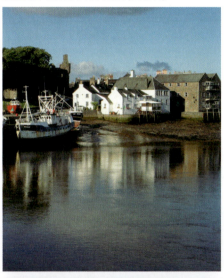

ABOVE: *Kirkcudbright waterfront (walk 3)*

BELOW: *Caerlaverock Castle (walk 11)*

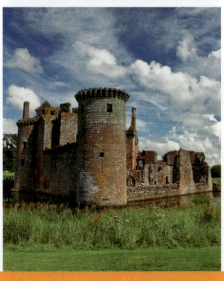

Walk locations and grades

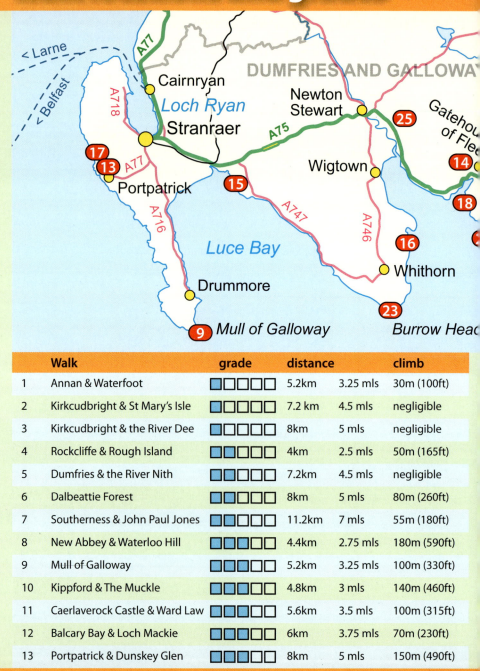

	Walk	grade		distance		climb
1	Annan & Waterfoot	■□□□□	5.2km	3.25 mls	30m (100ft)	
2	Kirkcudbright & St Mary's Isle	■□□□□	7.2 km	4.5 mls	negligible	
3	Kirkcudbright & the River Dee	■□□□□	8km	5 mls	negligible	
4	Rockcliffe & Rough Island	■■□□□	4km	2.5 mls	50m (165ft)	
5	Dumfries & the River Nith	■■□□□	7.2km	4.5 mls	negligible	
6	Dalbeattie Forest	■■□□□	8km	5 mls	80m (260ft)	
7	Southerness & John Paul Jones	■■□□□	11.2km	7 mls	55m (180ft)	
8	New Abbey & Waterloo Hill	■■■□□	4.4km	2.75 mls	180m (590ft)	
9	Mull of Galloway	■■■□□	5.2km	3.25 mls	100m (330ft)	
10	Kippford & The Muckle	■■■□□	4.8km	3 mls	140m (460ft)	
11	Caerlaverock Castle & Ward Law	■■■□□	5.6km	3.5 mls	100m (315ft)	
12	Balcary Bay & Loch Mackie	■■■□□	6km	3.75 mls	70m (230ft)	
13	Portpatrick & Dunskey Glen	■■■□□	8km	5 mls	150m (490ft)	

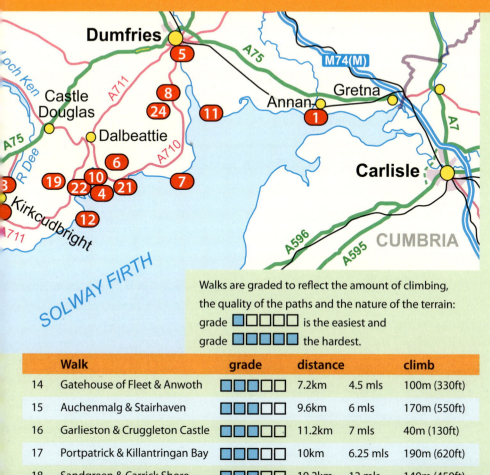

Walks are graded to reflect the amount of climbing, the quality of the paths and the nature of the terrain: grade ■□□□□ is the easiest and grade ■■■■■ the hardest.

	Walk	grade	distance		climb
14	Gatehouse of Fleet & Anwoth	■■□□□	7.2km	4.5 mls	100m (330ft)
15	Auchenmalg & Stairhaven	■■■□□	9.6km	6 mls	170m (550ft)
16	Garlieston & Cruggleton Castle	■■■□□	11.2km	7 mls	40m (130ft)
17	Portpatrick & Killantringan Bay	■■■□□	10km	6.25 mls	190m (620ft)
18	Sandgreen & Carrick Shore	■■■□□	19.2km	12 mls	140m (450ft)
19	Screel	■■■■□	6km	3.75 mls	350m (1150ft)
20	Brighouse Bay & Borness Fort	■■■■□	7.2km	4.5 mls	80m (260ft)
21	Kippford to Sandyhills	■■■■□	9.6km	6 mls	275m (900ft)
22	Palnackie & Almorness Point	■■■■□	14km	8.75 mls	140m (460ft)
23	Isle of Whithorn & St Ninian	■■■■■	17.2km	10.75 mls	170m (550ft)
24	Criffel & Knockendoch	■■■■■	12km	7.5 mls	590m (1930ft)
25	Cairnsmore of Fleet	■■■■■	19.2km	12 mls	1000m (3280ft)

Walks information and safety

For each walk, grid references are given in red for the start point and each numbered route point, as per the route map. These can be used with an Ordnance Survey map, or as GPS waypoints. Grid references are recognised by www.streetmap.co.uk, a map search website, which can show OS mapping.

The times given are approximate indications of how long walks will take, allowing a little time to look at things of interest.

This guide includes a map of every route, but for the more demanding walks (particularly walks 24 and 25), you are advised to carry a compass and full-sized map, which will show you more of the surrounding area and help with navigation if you stray from the route.

You should carry adequate equipment for your comfort and safety; consider taking a full set of waterproofs, spare warm clothing, food and drink, a torch and a whistle. It is sensible to let someone know when and where you are going, and your expected return time.

Weather can change rapidly on the coast and in the hills, and it is usually colder and windier higher up. In winter, ice and snow may make the going difficult or dangerous.

Take care on cliff walks, where steep drops are generally unprotected. They may be too dangerous to undertake in high winds. Keep children and dogs under close control.

On the Solway Firth the sea retreats a long way at low tide but comes back in very fast. Soft sand and mud may not support your weight, and shallow water can conceal deep, hidden channels. Check tide times before walking out to Rough Island (walk 4) or along beaches and rocky shores. Tide times can be found at http://news.bbc.co.uk/weather/coast_and_sea/tide_tables/. Select 'Scotland' then look at the bottom of the list for the few locations shown along the Galloway Coast.

OPPOSITE: *A blue-tailed damselfly*

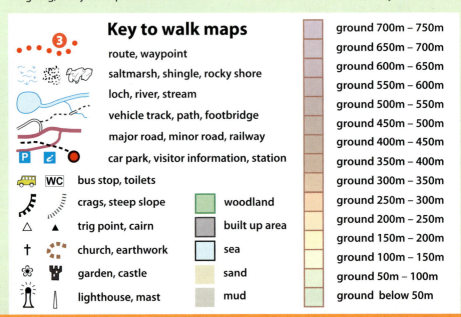

Key to walk maps

- route, waypoint
- saltmarsh, shingle, rocky shore
- loch, river, stream
- vehicle track, path, footbridge
- major road, minor road, railway
- car park, visitor information, station
- bus stop, toilets
- crags, steep slope
- trig point, cairn
- church, earthwork
- garden, castle
- lighthouse, mast

- woodland
- built up area
- sea
- sand
- mud

- ground 700m – 750m
- ground 650m – 700m
- ground 600m – 650m
- ground 550m – 600m
- ground 500m – 550m
- ground 450m – 500m
- ground 400m – 450m
- ground 350m – 400m
- ground 300m – 350m
- ground 250m – 300m
- ground 200m – 250m
- ground 150m – 200m
- ground 100m – 150m
- ground 50m – 100m
- ground below 50m

Nature Guide

Explore the natural world

The walks in this book will help you to explore the rich and varied natural heritage of the Galloway coast. They lead along cliff top paths above raucous seabird colonies, through woodlands that shelter deer, butterflies and wildflowers, and past saltmarshes where ducks, geese and waders feed.

What you see will be different through the seasons, as changing colours transform the landscape, and as birds and animals go through their natural cycles of breeding and migration. Even day to day, changing light and weather will create different views. The one constant you will find is that this is an unspoilt area where nature and people live in harmony.

Enjoy this special environment and please help to care for it, by leaving places as you find them and not causing disturbance or damage. Follow any reasonable advice and information you come across on the walks, keep your dog under proper control, and take your litter home.

Thanks to its position in the far southwest of Scotland, Dumfries and Galloway has a unique combination of plants and animals. The warming influence of the Gulf Stream enables colonies of rare species not found elsewhere in Scotland, such as the natterjack toad and pretty blue perennial flax, to thrive here. On the other hand, the black-throated divers and azure hawker dragonflies that breed here are at the southern limit of their range. As well as these specialities, the area is home to many of Scotland's iconic species, such as red deer, red squirrel, mountain hare, otter, osprey, puffin and red grouse.

The great diversity of habitats along the Galloway Coast allows many different plants and animals to find their own niche. The Solway Coast Heritage Trail, a waymarked driving route that includes many of the walk locations, highlights this diversity. The booklet can be downloaded as a pdf file from **www.dgerc.org.uk**.

ABOVE: *Puffins can be seen during the breeding season at the Mull of Galloway (walk 9).*

LEFT: *Common toadflax (photographed on walk 23, Isle of Whithorn).*

Wildlife watching

This nature guide highlights some of the exciting wildlife that can be experienced through the seasons on the walks. The following pages describe a few of the more conspicuous birds and wildflowers you may see along the Galloway coast, as well as the various habitats in which they live. It is not intended to be a comprehensive wildlife handbook; for more information consult specialist field guides.

Spring is when deciduous woods are carpeted in wildflowers before the young green leaves open. Frogs and toads lay their spawn and the first butterflies emerge. Birds of prey and songbirds are busy feeding their young, while seabirds return to land to claim their nest sites.

Summer brings a vivid flush of colour to coast and hill as wildflowers bloom. Butterflies and dragonflies flit over the lush vegetation. Seabird colonies are a hive of activity with fish constantly being brought to feed the fluffy chicks.

Autumn sees a major influx of wildfowl and waders, which come from northern climes to feed on the food-rich coast during the relatively mild winter. Nuts and berries ripen, and woods and grassland are burnished with autumn colours.

Winter is a spectacular time of year for migrant ducks, geese, swans and wading birds, some of which do not depart until April, when the snow has thawed on their breeding grounds. It is easier to see woodland species, such as red squirrel and tree creeper, on the leafless trees.

TOP: *Red deer, the largest wild land mammals in Galloway, live in the mountain areas; stags grow new antlers each year.*

UPPER MIDDLE: *Both the grey seal and smaller common seal are seen along the coast. Dolphins, porpoises and whales may be spotted from the clifftop walks.*

LOWER MIDDLE: *In April, mating toads walk overland to breed in Caerlaverock Castle moat (walk 11) and other ponds.*

BOTTOM: *One of our rarer butterflies, the Scotch argus is found in rough, boggy grassland in wild parts of Galloway.*

Birds

1 Herring gull: seen all along the coast, this large gull has a fierce look and a noisy call. Adults have flesh coloured legs and a yellow bill with a red spot near the end. Juveniles are mottled brown. Eats almost anything.

4 Razorbill: a smart black and white seabird with a heavy, blunt bill and a white line running up to the eye. It nests colonially in crevices in cliffs or between boulders. Spending most of the year at sea, it feeds mainly on fish.

7 Common tern: swallow-like seabird that hovers over the sea before diving for fish. It lays two or three eggs in a shallow scrape in shingle or sand. Like the similar Arctic tern, it will dive-bomb intruders near the nest site.

10 Barnacle goose: over 25,000 migrate from the Arctic in October and stay on the Solway coast until early April, feeding on saltmarsh, pasture and arable crops. They have a creamy white face and delicate bill.

13 Peregrine: this large and powerful falcon preys on birds, out-flying and catching them on the wing. It nests on sea cliffs, where it hunts seabirds, as well as inland on mountain crags and quarries.

2 Kittiwake: a small, neat gull with a yellow bill and short black legs. Its name is derived from the sound of its call. Only coming to land to breed in colonies on cliff ledges, it makes a small cup-shaped nest of mud.

5 Guillemot: has a dark brown back and head with a thin, tapered bill. Breeding colonies crowd together on narrow cliff ledges that are splashed white with 'guano'. The egg is laid on bare rock and constantly guarded.

8 Shag: looks like a cormorant, but lacks the white face-patch and does not venture inland. It has a greenish tinge to its plumage and a small crest in summer. The nest, low on a cliff, is composed of flotsam.

11 Whooper swan: (front) is a winter visitor and has a yellow and black bill, unlike the orange and black bill of the resident mute swan (rear). Coming mainly from Iceland, they feed in shallow water and on grassland.

14 Red kite: is more agile in the air than the similar sized buzzard. It eats mainly carrion and small mammals. Successfully reintroduced to Scotland after being persecuted to extinction, it roosts communally in winter.

3 Fulmar: appears gull-like but has more rapid, stiff wing beats and glides effortlessly. Its distinctive beak has tube-like nostrils. It lays a single egg on a vegetated ledge and is largely silent, except when greeting its mate.

6 Puffin: recognised by its colourful bill and bright orange feet, it is surprisingly small. Colonies nest in holes on the grassy upper reaches of cliffs, often in old rabbit burrows. The young are fed mainly on sand eels.

9 Oystercatcher: the most conspicuous of the many waders found along the coast, it often flies overhead piping noisily. Uses its long, orange-red bill to probe for cockles and lugworms, and nests on open ground.

12 Shelduck: is a large, white duck with a bottle-green head, chestnut breast band and black wing-tips. It nests secretively in holes or vegetation, and feeds in sheltered bays and estuaries with mudbanks.

15 Barn owl: hunts silently at night over farmland and coastal marshes, catching voles, mice and shrews. Its call is a piercing shriek. Nesting in barns, caves or hollow trees, it lays eggs on a bed of regurgitated pellets.

Wildflowers

1 Oysterplant: this rare plant grows in a few places along the coast, forming a mat on shoreline shingle. The flowers turn from pink to blue-purple. The fleshy, greyish-green leaves are supposed to taste of oysters.

4 Thrift: or sea pink is common on sea cliffs, rocks and saltmarshes and inland on mountains. The roundish flower heads grow profusely from clumps of grass-like leaves and bleach from dark pink to pale pink.

7 Harebell: sometimes called the 'Scottish bluebell', is a delicate looking but surprisingly hardy plant of dry grassland. The hanging, bell-shaped blue flowers grow on long, thin stalks and survive clifftop winds.

10 Bluebell: the fragrant, bell-shaped flowers grow on a one-sided spike above the linear leaves. Forms dense patches in woods and on steep banks above the sea, creating a purply-blue haze when in bloom around May.

13 Cuckoo flower: also called lady's smock, grows in wet grassland and has pale lilac or white flowers from April to June. A member of the cabbage family, it is the main foodstuff of orange tip butterfly caterpillars.

2 Sea aster: is a short, fleshy perennial of saltmarshes and sea cliffs. Its daisy-shaped flowers grow in loose clusters and have a yellow centre with pale purple rays. They can be seen from July to October.

5 Sea campion: is related to the common red campion of woods and meadows, but is white and has a distinctive bladder below the petals, formed by an inflated sepal tube. Summer flowering, it grows on cliffs and shingle.

8 Gorse: this evergreen shrub with prickly, spiny leaves thrives on heaths and clifftops. The yellow, coconut-scented flowers can be seen in any month, but peak in April. Small birds nest within its cover.

11 Wood anemone: grows in deciduous woods and flowers March to April before trees come into leaf and shade it. The leaves are long-stalked and deeply-lobed and the white flowers are often pinkish underneath.

14 Yellow iris: the large, showy flowers rise above the long sword-shaped leaves and open in June. It is plant of marshy ground beside fresh water, and is often seen by streams where they meet the shore.

3 Sea sandwort: easily missed, this creeping plant forms a carpet of fleshy, yellow-green leaves. Tiny white star-like flowers are dotted amid the leaves from May to August. Its fruit looks like a small green pea.

6 English stonecrop: grows in a low mat over bare cliffs and rock. It has fleshy leaves that retain moisture in the sun, and start green but soon turn red. Pretty little pinkish-white flowers appear from June to September.

9 Juniper: a rare native conifer, it grows as an small evergreen shrub or tree. It has grey-green needle-like leaves and separate male and female plants. The berry-like cones turn black and are used to flavour gin.

12 Wood sorrel: is smaller and more delicate than the wood anemone. It grows in similar places, often among moss. The white flowers are veined mauve and the clover-shaped leaves are a bright, yellowish green.

15 Heath spotted orchid: one of several orchids found in Galloway, it grows on acidic heaths and bogs and blooms in summer. The two-lipped flowers grow on a stalked spike, above the lance-shaped spotted leaves.

Coastal habitats

◄ Cliffs form where higher, harder rocks resist erosion by the sea, as in Galloway along much of the western coast. They are home in spring and summer to nesting seabirds that lay eggs and raise their young on ledges and in crevices. Different species have their own preferred sites, with puffins and fulmars near the top, guillemots and kittiwakes on ledges midway up the cliffs, and shags low down near the splash zone.

Clifftops are exposed to wind and salt ▶ spray, making them a hostile environment for most wildlife. The pretty blue spring squill specialises in growing on the short maritime heath, and pink cushions of thrift and nodding harebells thrive on the thin turf. Where the cliffs are less exposed to westerly gales, yellow-flowering gorse and wind-bent hawthorn take hold, providing habitat for the tuneful linnet and twite.

◄ Beaches are very dynamic environments – where land and sea meet and mingle. They may be composed of sand, shingle, pebbles or even shells, depending on the local geology and what the currents bring onshore. Regular inundation by the sea makes beaches a difficult place for wildlife, but ringed plovers and terns nest near the high tide mark, where specialist wildflowers such as oysterplant can also gain a foothold.

Rocky shores may at first appear devoid ▶ of life, but look closer and you can find miniature worlds in the rock pools left by the retreating tide. Sea anemones, shrimps, small fish and vivid seaweed survive in these pools, while limpets and bladder wrack cling to the rocks. Even the rock itself is coloured by the lichens living on them: black where they are constantly being wetted, then grey, pale green and orange higher up the shore.

Sand dunes occur where strong winds blow loose sand into heaps behind a beach. Where stabilised by marram grass, wildflowers like sea sandwort can take hold. Eventually grassland and heath develops on the mounds, often with small pools in the hollows providing breeding sites for dragonflies and the rare natterjack toad. The sun baked environment is ideal for common lizards and butterflies.

Saltmarsh or **Merse**, as it is known locally, is found mainly along the lower lying eastern coast, although smaller areas exist in many of the sheltered bays. Occurring where the sea periodically floods flat land, it is covered by a sward of salt tolerant grasses and wildflowers, such as sea spurrey and scurvy-grass, separated by muddy channels. Thousands of geese and swans graze the merse during the winter.

◄ **Mudflats** and **Sandbanks** extend for miles across the upper Solway Firth, where sediments are constantly shifted by tides and added to by particles borne by rivers. The mud is full of tiny creatures that provide rich feeding for waders, such as curlew, redshank and knot. Cockle pickers work far out from land, braving fast incoming tides, while stake nets were traditionally stretched across the sand to catch salmon.

Estuaries offer shelter and food for a vast array of wildlife, from invertebrates and young fish to herons and otters. Here fresh and saltwater mix, and vegetation often comes right down to the shore. The shallows are warmed by the sun, creating a productive environment. Ospreys find the relatively unruffled waters excellent for catching fish, and large rafts of ducks over-winter in the protected bays.

Freshwater habitats

Rivers in Galloway tend not to be very long as they soon reach the sea, but their clean waters support salmon and many other species of fish. Herons stalk along their edges and kingfishers flash between perches. The rivers are often fringed by willow and alder, trees that like to have their roots wet, or by reeds and lush vegetation, such as meadowsweet, purple loosestrife and yellow irises.

◀ **Burns** are usually clear and fast flowing, with rock or gravel beds in their upper reaches. They provide corridors of habitat for otters and water voles, as well as water-loving plants like marsh marigold and water forget-me-not. The white-breasted dipper specialises in walking underwater to feed on the insect larvae, while the yellow-breasted grey wagtail flits about after hatching flies. Salmon and trout spawn in many burns.

◀ **Lochs** are smaller and shallower here than in Highland Scotland, but often richer in wildlife. Goldeneye and tufted ducks dive for food in the open water, while dragonflies and damselflies hunt along their marshy edges. The surrounding vegetation is home to willow tits and warblers, as well as many species of butterfly. Larger lochs provide safe roost sites for wintering greylag and pink-footed geese.

Wetlands may be increasingly rare, but there are plenty of undrained areas in Galloway that provide invaluable habitat. Orchids, cuckoo flower, ragged robin and marsh lousewort turn damp ground into a kaleidoscope of colour, while sedge warbler and reed bunting fill the air with their repetitive calls. Ducks, such as teal and widgeon feed on flooded areas, and at dusk barn owls and roe deer silently appear.

Native woodland along the coast is predominately oak, which was often coppiced in the past. It includes a wide mix of birch, hazel, ash, willow, alder, rowan, and other broadleaved species depending on soils, drainage and aspect. Their foliage is fresh green in spring, and turns gold, russet and bronze in autumn. The understory is rich in mosses and spring wildflowers, such as wood sorrel, primrose and bluebell.

Wood pasture is how much of the landscape was managed in the past and can still be seen in many places across the area. It is a non-intensive way of combining grazing for cattle or sheep with management of trees and scrub. As well as providing shelter for livestock, such as these native long-horned cattle, it benefits biodiversity. The unimproved grassland is herb-rich and supports a wealth of insects and birds.

Conifer forests in Galloway are planted for commercial production of timber, but are also used for recreation and by wildlife. Scots pine and juniper, the only conifers native here, are much less widespread than Sitka spruce and other introduced conifers grown in large plantations on less fertile land. Butterflies and wildflowers colonise track verges and clearings, while siskins, crossbills and coal tits feed in the forest canopy.

Policy woods are planted on farms and estates, particularly around big houses. Often they are a key part of designed landscapes laid out a century or two ago, and typically feature mature broadleaved trees, interspersed with specimen conifers, such as firs and redwoods. Fine stands of beech trees or other single species are common, sometimes planted in avenues or roundels.

Hill and farmand habitats

◀ **Hills** are covered with heather moorland in higher, more acidic areas. Blooming in late summer, the heather is intermixed with blaeberry (bilberry), cowberry and bog cotton. Peregrine and merlin hunt over moorland where wheatear and meadow pipit nest. Lower down, rough grassland is speckled with tormentil, milkwort and wild thyme, with lousewort, butterwort and bog asphodel flowering on wet flushes.

Heathland is often lightly grazed, which ▶ keeps it as open habitat where skylarks sing overhead and stonechats scold from shrubby bushes. Birdsfoot trefoil, violets and heath bedstraw grow through the grass, but can be shaded out by bracken. Sunny spots are used by basking lizards and adders. It is important habitat for butterflies, such as the northern brown argus and small pearl-bordered fritillary.

◀ **Pasture** is grassland specifically managed for grazing livestock and is one of Galloway's most noticeable features. There are miles of rolling green fields, which grow lush in the mild, damp climate. The grass fattens beef cattle and gives dairy cows plentiful milk. Fewer wildflowers grow in pasture 'improved' by reseeding and fertiliser, though you will still see buttercups, daisies, dandelions and clover.

Cropped land is found mainly in eastern ▶ parts, where deeper, richer soils are used to grow cereals and vegetables for human consumption or livestock feed. Pesticides make these the least bio-diverse areas, although even here wildflowers of disturbed ground, such as poppies and scentless mayweed, appear around field edges. The hedgerows between fields are particularly important for insects and birds.

Places to visit

ABOVE: *Thousands of Barnacle Geese and other wildfowl overwinter at Caerlaverock National Nature Reserve (walk 11) and are easily viewed from the hides at the Wildfowl and Wetlands Trust Centre.*

Keep your eyes and ears open, and you will see and hear lots of wildlife on the walks in this book. The routes visit some very special places, including the National Nature Reserves at Caerlaverock (walk 11) and Cairnsmore of Fleet (walk 25); the Mull of Galloway Special Area of Conservation (walk 9); and Sites of Special Scientific Interest such as Port o' Warren (walk 21), the Borgue Coast (walk 20) and Burrow Head (walk 23).

There are also many excellent sites near the walks for seeing wildflowers, birds, and other animals in their natural habitat. They include ancient woodlands and Wigtown Bay, Britain's largest Local Nature Reserve. From east to west, here are some well worth visiting.

Caerlaverock NNR, Wildfowl & Wetlands Trust Centre: Mudflats and saltmarsh. Visitor centre at Eastpark Farm, NY051656, tel. 01387 770200, www.wwt.org.uk.

Mabie Forest:
Planted mixed woodland with mountain bike trails, bike hire, walks and café, NX950710, tel. 01387 860247, www.forestry.gov.uk.

Mersehead RSPB Nature Reserve:
Wetlands, saltmarsh, woodland and farmland. Visitor centre near Caulkerbush at NX928566, tel. 01387 780579, www.rspb.org.uk.

Ken-Dee Marshes RSPB Reserve:
River, loch and marsh, north of Glenlochar. Parking at NX699684, tel. 01556 670464, www.rspb.org.uk.

Galloway Kite Trail:
24-mile route around Loch Ken with red kite information, walks, viewing hides and feeding station, www.gallowaykitetrail.com.

Carstramon Wood, SWT Reserve:
Ancient oak wood with paths. Parking north of Gatehouse of Fleet at NX589600, www.scottishwildlifetrust.org.uk.

Cairnsmore of Fleet NNR:
Mountain and moorland. Visitor centre at Dromore, NX554637, 10 miles from walk 25, tel. 01557 814435, www.nnr-scotland.org.uk.

Wood of Cree RSPB reserve:
Ancient native woodland with a network of trails. Parking at NX381708, north of Newton Stewart, tel. 01988 402130, www.rspb.org.uk.

Glentrool, Galloway Forest Park:
Visitor centre at NX372786 is the gateway to Loch Trool and the highest Galloway hills, tel. 01671 840302, www.gallowayforestpark.com.

Wigtown Bay LNR:
Saltmarsh and mudflats with bird hides and council visitor centre. Parking at NX438546, tel. 01988 402401, www.dumgal.gov.uk.

Mull of Galloway RSPB Reserve:
Sea cliffs and coastal heath with nature trail, tearoom and visitor centre at NX156305, tel. 01988 402130, www.rspb.org.uk.

National Scenic Areas

Dumfries and Galloway contains three of Scotland's National Scenic Areas (NSAs). All three lie along the coast of the Solway Firth. This designation recognises their outstanding natural beauty and protects them as part of Scotland's heritage. Many walks in this book explore these areas, which contain particularly attractive landscapes and are home to some of Scotland's most important wildflowers and animals.

Around the Nith Estuary, a dramatic combination of land, sea and sky gives the scenery a bold, elemental quality. It is a big, open landscape with panoramic views across the Solway Firth to the coast of Cumbria. The great mass of Criffel (walk 24) towers above the shore, contrasting with the flat expanses of mudflats and saltmarsh adjacent to Caerlaverock Castle (walk 11). Sweetheart Abbey (walk 8) adds a human element to the view and is set amid rolling, green farmland that is a living, working landscape.

By contrast, the East Stewartry Coast is a sheltered, enclosed area, where promontories and islands protect shallow bays that dry out at low tide. The indented coastline and irregular topography keep the views small scale and create a sense of intimacy. The Almorness peninsula near Palnackie (walk 22) separates Auchencairn Bay from Rough Firth, which is bisected by Rough Island and its causeway (walk 4). In many places woodland comes right down to the shore, as around Kippford (walk 10).

Beyond the bays, the coastline exposed to the open sea has wave sculpted cliffs with sea stacks and natural arches, as seen at Balcary Point (walk 12) and between the prehistoric fort at Castlehill Point and the lovely beach at Sandyhills (walk 21). All this complex scene is overlooked by Screel (walk 19), which offers the most wonderful views.

The **Fleet Valley** has a remarkable mix of landscape types that progress, within a short distance, from coastal scenery to hills and mountains. Well managed farmland and broadleaf woodland provide a distinctive setting for the historic planned town of Gatehouse of Fleet (walk 14). It sits at the high tide mark on the Water of Fleet, midway between the head of the valley and the Islands of Fleet, which lie off Sandgreen and Carrick (walk 18). The summit of Cairnsmore of Fleet (walk 25) offers a panoramic view over this National Scenic Area.

ABOVE LEFT: *Location of the National Scenic Areas*

BELOW LEFT: *Nith Esturary from the summit of Knockendoch (walk 24)*

ABOVE: *East Stewartry Coast from Screel (walk 19), with the Lake District mountains and Robin Rigg wind farm – on a mid Solway sandbank – in the distance*

BELOW: *Fleet Valley from the Samuel Rutherford Monument above Gatehouse of Fleet (walk 14)*

Geology

LEFT: *Rock and sand meet at Sandyhills beach where cliffs give way to saltmarsh and sand dunes (walk 21)*

OPPOSITE: *Southerness Lighthouse is built on sedimentary rocks from the Carboniferous period (walk 7)*

The landscapes of the Galloway Coast reflect their underlying geology. The type of rock and how it erodes determines the shape of land forms and what can grow.

On many walks you will see lush green pastures, undulating over low ridges and hills. These knolls are usually orientated southwest to northeast, the same alignment as the tilted strata of the underlying rock, which is often exposed on the shore. This is most apparent on walks 18 and 23. The rock is greywacke, a hard sandstone, that is the bedrock of most of Galloway. It has ancient origins, having been deposited by turbidity currents in warm seas around **450 million years ago**, during the late Ordovician and early Silurian periods, when Scotland lay in the tropics. It is resistant to erosion, but grass grows very well on the thin soils it produces.

The high, rounded hills of Cairnsmore of Fleet (walk 25) and Criffel (walk 24) are composed of granite – a rough rock, speckled with large mineral crystals. This formed about **400 million years ago**, during the Devonian period, when the movement of tectonic plates caused large masses of molten magma to rise into the earth's crust, where they solidified deep underground. Granite is hard but eventually erodes, creating acidic, nutrient-poor soils, on which only moorland plants such as blaeberry and heather thrive.

Along the shore between Southerness and Arbigland (walk 7), are layers of sedimentary rocks laid down in shallow seas about **360-300 million years ago**, during the Carboniferous period. They consist of fossil-bearing mudstones, siltstones and thick beds of sandstone – one at the Thirlstane Arch is 15 metres deep.

The red sandstone buildings that characterise Dumfries (walk 5) and Annan (walk 1) town centres are evidence that Scotland had a desert landscape around **300 to 250 million years ago**, during the Permian period. The rocks along the eastern part of the coast were formed from ancient sand dunes. This sandstone produces some the most fertile soils in the region.

From about **2.5 million to 12,000 years ago**, Scotland went through several Ice Ages, which left their mark on the landscape. Glaciers carved deep, U-shaped glens through the hills and deposited mounds of meltwater gravel on the valley floors of the Rivers Annan, Dee and Nith (walks 1, 3 and 5).

Walks

1

This gentle walk follows the River Annan downstream from the town centre, past wharves where Robert Burns worked as an exciseman, to tidal salt marshes on the Solway Firth.

Annan & Waterfoot

Start	War memorial, High Street, Annan **NY194665**
Grade	■☐☐☐☐
Distance	5.2km (3.25 miles)
Ascent	30m (100ft)
Time	2 hours
Terrain	Pavement, riverside and coastal paths, minor roads.

Getting there: Annan is 15.5 miles east of Dumfries, via the A75. There are several car parks within the town near the start.

Public transport: Regular Scotrail services from Dumfries to Annan and regular Stagecoach Bus Service 379 Dumfries to Annan.

The River Annan begins its journey at the base of Hart Fell near Moffat, eventually flowing into the Solway Firth at Annan. The river is noted for its salmon, brown trout and sea trout fishing. During autumn salmon can be seen moving up river to spawn whilst otters, kingfisher, heron and red squirrels are frequent visitors along the river.

Annan was granted Royal Burgh status in the 13th Century by the Bruce family, who were Lords of Annandale. Annan then established itself as a market town with shipbuilding and sandstone quarrying amongst its industries. Certainly, the first thing that catches the eye are the fine red sandstone buildings, which include the Town Hall, post office and library, and the wonderful road and railway bridges that span the River Annan.

Waterfoot was a successful port between 1780 and 1848 when emigrants sailed from here to North America on schooners or brigs. Two 128-metre long jetties were constructed in 1819, but in 1848 all the traffic transferred to the newly open railway system. In the early 1790s Robert Burns worked at Waterfoot as an excise man and during this time wrote his poem *The Deil's Awa' wi' the Exciseman.*

This simple stroll from Annan to Waterfoot follows easily navigable minor roads, riverbank and coastal paths. The mudbanks along the Solway Firth are home to a fine selection of wading birds and Waterfoot offers exceptional views of the Lake District.

LEFT: *Annan Town Hall (point 1)*

1 **NY194665** From the War Memorial on High Street, walk towards the tall clock tower of the striking Town Hall, which was built in 1878. Cross High Street here then go right, across Port Street, and continue over Annan Road Bridge, which spans the lovely River Annan. At the end of the bridge turn left down a flight of steps (signposted for Barnkirk Point) onto a riverside path.

2 **NY191666** Walk along the path above the river and just before a metal footbridge turn right onto the Annandale Way (also a cycle-track) and follow this as it spirals up left to take you back across the River Annan, via the footbridge, giving a great view of the marvellous archways of the railway bridge. Once over the bridge continue straight on around a barrier onto Riverside Walk. Follow the pavement until you reach the junction with Port Street.

3 **NY189664** Turn right, walk along Port Street underneath the railway bridge to reach the old Burgh Quay. Just before the harbour turn left into a lane, which leads to Waterfoot Road. Turn right and follow the road away from Annan. It narrows to a single-track road and reaches a gate beside a cattle grid – go through and continue along the road, through peaceful countryside. Pass a memorial cairn to Robert Burns and reach the coastal marshland of Waterfoot, where you can enjoy terrific views of Cumbria, which is only about one mile away across the Solway Firth. The track leads down to the shore where oystercatcher and curlew are in abundance.

4 **NY191646** Retrace your steps back onto the track and pass the cairn. After a few metres, bear right onto a path signposted for Whinnyrig and follow this raised path above the coastal grassland through a line of hawthorn trees onto a lane, which passes a couple of houses.

5 **NY192650** At a junction, turn left onto a single-track road, which climbs gently past some houses away from the coast and then swings right onto Argyll Terrace and continues onto Sutherland Terrace and then Gordon Terrace. Follow the pavement past more houses with some great views along the coast.

6 **NY194654** The road then bears left and climbs gently, giving a good view towards Annan, before dropping down into Elm Road where the pavement ends. Near Elmvale Primary School rejoin the pavement. Elm Road then crosses the railway line by a bridge and here it becomes Station Road. Follow the main road as it swings right into St John's Road then fork left into Bank Street. At the junction with High Street, turn left back to the start.

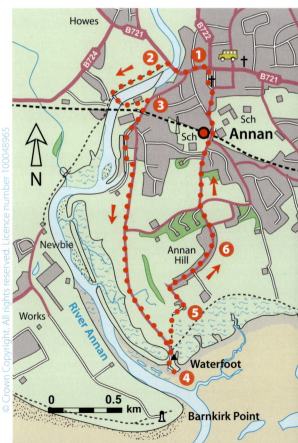

2

This peaceful peninsula, which was for centuries a monastic retreat from the world, has wonderful views over Kirkcudbright Bay and is a haven for wildlife.

Kirkcudbright & St Mary's Isle

Start	Kirkcudbright Harbour **NX683511**
Grade	■□□□□
Distance	7.2km (4.5 miles)
Ascent	Negligible
Time	2 hours
Terrain	Pavement and woodland paths.

Getting there: Kirkcudbright is 9.5 miles southwest of Castle Douglas via the A75 and A711. Turn right into St Cuthbert Street after the A755 Bridge Street junction then right into the car park.
Public transport: Regular Stagecoach Service 502 bus service from Castle Douglas to Kirkcudbright.

ABOVE: Walking through autumn woodland on St Mary's Isle (point 3)

A walk through Kirkcudbright leads to the wooded peninsula of St Mary's Isle where an excellent path circuits the peninsula. There are several offshoot paths leading down to the shore, but care should be taken at high tide and also at low tide when rocky ground and mudflats are exposed.

MacLellan's Castle stands at the corner of Castle Street and St Cuthbert Street, and dominates Kirkcudbright's harbourside. After the Reformation of 1560 the Convent of Greyfriars was abandoned and the Provost, Sir Thomas MacLellan, acquired the lands. Using stone from the convent and the old royal castle, MacLellan's Castle was completed in 1582.

St Mary's Isle was once separated from the mainland at high tide. It had a priory for Augustinian Canons who served a semi-monastic life here between the 14th and 16th centuries. After the Reformation it ceased to function as a monastery. It is believed that Robert Burns composed the *Selkirk Grace* whilst visiting the Earl of Selkirk at St Mary's Isle.

The isle's lovely woodland is renowned for its snowdrops, whilst the shore provides feeding for redshank, curlew and heron. From **5**, you can see Little Ross, an island at the mouth of Kirkudbright Bay. In 1960, a father and son who sailed there found the body of a lighthouse keeper. After a nationwide hunt his fellow keeper was arrested, found guilty of murder and sentenced to hang.

1 **NX683511** From the harbour walk through the car park onto St Cuthbert's Street (with McLellan's Castle just a short distance to the right). Turn left along the street then turn right onto St Mary's Street (the A711). Pass several of Kirkcudbright's fine buildings, including the Town Hall and Kirkcudbright Parish Church, and follow the pavement over Daar Road and then past the marvellous Stewartry Museum, which is well worth a visit. Cross over High Street, and once over Castledykes Road, go straight ahead onto a single-track road, passing through a gate and onto St Mary's Isle.

2 **NX683505** Leaving the hustle and bustle of Kirkcudbright behind, follow this quiet road, lined by beech and sycamore, passing several houses. After the road swings right and passes a driveway leading to a house, take a narrow path branching right from the road into woodland.

3 **NX679501** Follow the path to a fence from where it turns left and hugs the coastline of St Mary's Isle, running beside coastal grassland where cows graze and oystercatchers probe for invertebrates. It is an excellent path with lots of wildflowers and some fine views along Kirkcudbright Bay. At a fork go left (the right fork leads a short distance down to a beach) and continue along the path through woodland, listening out for woodpeckers, to a broader track.

4 **NX669490** Continue along the track, passing the remains of an old harbour, to reach the point of the peninsula. As the track swings left, a narrow, indistinct path on the right leads down to a quiet beach. Here the view extends past the little wooded island of Inch to Little Ross lighthouse. Look for waders searching for food on the mudflats.

5 **NX670483** Retrace your steps to the main track, turn right and continue through woodland around the peninsula. The track swings left by Paul Jones Point. Once past a house, turn right onto a single-track road and follow this wildflower-lined way, where red campion and heath spotted orchid grow in abundance.

6 **NX676493** Pass a turning to the left and follow the road beside a lovely open field to reach another road. Turn right along it, with good views to Kirkcudbright.

7 **NX683500** On reaching the A711, turn left, walk along the pavement and follow it into Kirkcudbright. Turn left at St Cuthbert's Street to return to the harbour.

3

The picturesque town of Kirkcudbright lies a few miles downstream from the Red Kite Trail on the River Dee; the tidal stretch to Tongland abounds in heron, ducks and waders.

Kirkcudbright & the River Dee

Start	MacLellan's Castle, Kirkcudbright **NX682509**
Grade	☐☐☐☐☐
Distance	8km (5 miles)
Ascent	Negligible
Time	2 hours
Terrain	Pavement and riverside paths.

Getting there: Kirkcudbright is 9.5 miles southwest of Castle Douglas via the A75 and A711. Turn right into St Cuthbert Street after the A755 Bridge Street junction then right into the car park.
Public transport: Regular Stagecoach Service 502 bus service from Castle Douglas to Kirkcudbright.

Kirkcudbright is named after the Kirk of St Cuthbert. A monastery was established here around 1000AD, and a royal castle, an Augustinian priory and a Franciscan friary all followed over the subsequent centuries. The town gained Royal Burgh status in 1455 mainly due to its harbour and the important trade links this bestowed. However, it was the scenic quality of the town and surrounding landscape, as well as the quality of light, that began to attract artists in the 19th century. Today Kirkcudbright is known as *The Artists' Town*, with many artists living and exhibiting here.

Well-maintained paths are used on this route, which follows the course of the attractive River Dee upstream to Tongland, passing the Thomas Telford designed Tongland Bridge. The Dee, which begins its journey only 15 miles away at Loch Ken, is tidal here. At low tide, the textured mud banks are exposed with the like of curlew, redshank and oystercatcher enjoying the consequent feeding opportunities. Most of the return journey uses the outward path.

Tongland straddles the Dee a couple of miles upstream from Kirkcudbright. Its name is derived from the Norse Tungland, meaning strip of land and, between 1134 and 1140, Fergus Lord of Galloway built Tongland Abbey here for the Premonstratensian monastic community. The Dee was dammed at this point in the 1930s as part of the Galloway Hydroelectric scheme, which has supplied electricity to the National Grid since 1935.

ABOVE: *View across the River Dee to Cumstoun House (between points 3 & 4)*

❶ NX682509 Facing MacLellan's Castle at the corner of Castle Street and St Cuthbert Street, go down Castle Bank (with the castle on your left). Turn right at Harbour Cottage Gallery to reach the harbour. Walk to the right along the quayside to pick up a path, which runs parallel to Beaconsfield Place. Follow this to Bridge Street (A755).

❷ NX685512 Cross Bridge Street and pick up a good path, which runs above the River Dee beside Dee Walk, and follow it past Kirkcudbright Lifeboat Station. At the end of Dee Walk go through a gate, bear right into parkland and follow the path away from Kirkcudbright passing some fine villas. The Dee looks superb as it snakes its way through the landscape.

❸ NX690522 Cross a footbridge, turn left and continue along the path between hedgerows and trees above the Dee. There are great views over lovely open countryside and across the Dee to Cumstoun House, which was built in 1828 by the architect Thomas Hamilton. He also designed The Royal High School on Edinburgh's Calton Hill.

❹ NX690532 Still following the Dee, the path then enters a lovely short strip of oak and beech woodland with a steep drop to the river on the left. Follow the path to Tongland Bridge. Go through a gate, cross the A711 then go through a second gate onto a wide grassy track, which runs along a field edge.

❺ NX692533 Follow the track under the archway of an old railway viaduct. Go left at a fork, making your way above the Dee and passing some lovely oak trees and an old fort. At a gate where you can see the Tongland Power Station, go through onto a narrow wooded path that climbs gradually. Cross over a stile then continue on the path high above the Dee with the impressive structure of the power station directly across the river. The path then descends to another fine stone bridge at Culdoach Road.

❻ NX696537 Turn left to cross the bridge over the Dee and follow the road (there is no pavement here) to reach the A711 in Tongland. Turn left onto a pavement, which runs beside the A711 high above the River Dee. Pass the power station and continue back to Tongland Bridge.

❼ NX692534 Cross the bridge then turn right across the A711 and go through the gate onto the outward path. Retrace your steps, enjoying great views along the Dee to Kirkcudbright all the way back to the town centre.

4

The National Trust for Scotland owns and protects much of the land in this area, allowing wildlife, such as red squirrels, redstarts and the northern brown argus butterfly, to flourish.

Rockcliffe & Rough Island

Start	Rockcliffe Upper Car Park **NX852536**
Grade	◼️◻️◻️◻️◻️
Distance	4km (2.5 miles)
Ascent	50m (165ft)
Time	1.5 hours
Terrain	Pavement, sand, causeway and paths. Rough Island is only accessible at low tide, which occurs twice a day for several hours at a time.

Getting there: Rockcliffe is 1 mile off the A710, 7 miles southeast of Dalbeattie and 21 miles southwest of Dumfries.

Public transport: Regular Stagecoach buses Service 372A from Dalbeattie to Rockcliffe.

ABOVE: *View along the casueway towards Kippford from Rough Island (point 3)*

Rough Island has been owned by the National Trust for Scotland since 1937. It is an RSPB nature reserve. The island lies 0.5km off Rockcliffe and can be walked to at low tide. It rises to 24m in height, affording a wonderful view along the Rough Firth to Kippford, and across the Solway Firth to Scafell Pike in the Lake District. The island is an important breeding ground for species such as oystercatcher and ringed plover, and therefore the island cannot be visited during May, June and early July to avoid disturbing any nests.

Rockcliffe: People have lived and worked in this vicinity for several millennia, with nearby Castlehill Point and Mote of Mark containing remains of Iron Age forts. During the Victorian era the village became a popular tourist destination and this status continues today – certainly during the summer the area is busy with many holiday makers enjoying the lovely beaches, coastline and attractive woodland.

Although Rough Island is easily reached at low tide, a close eye must be kept on the sea level at all times. The speed at which the tide comes in can easily be underestimated and has caught many people out. Check tide times before starting (see page 10). Please avoid this walk during the bird nesting season.

1 **NX852536** From the car park, turn left onto Millbrae and walk down the pavement, crossing Merse Road. Continue above the shore to a slipway at Rockcliffe beach.

2 **NX848537** Turn left and descend the slipway. Go straight down the beach and through an obvious gap in the rocks onto firmer sand, heading towards Rough Island, which lies directly ahead. Once beyond the rocky shoreline, bear right and cross the sand towards the northern tip of the island. Cross a narrow channel and continue to a shingly beach beside a causeway. The causeway is a prominent bank of shells and sand that has been shaped by the tides.

3 **NX843534** At the causeway, turn left onto Rough Island, and join a path beside a National Trust sign. The narrow path goes through a short section of elder and hawthorn trees then climbs quite steeply over a meadow, which is bursting with wildflowers during spring and summer. Continue to the cairn on Rough Island's summit, which is a great place to sit. Here the views towards Rockcliffe, Castlehill Point and the Lake District are magnificent.

4 **NX845531** Retrace your steps to the causeway and walk along it back onto the mainland. Go up an obvious shell beach on the outskirts of Kippford and turn left onto a single-track road. Follow this for a short distance past some impressive stone villas to a track on the right signposted for Rockcliffe.

5 **NX841542** Follow this track, which quickly narrows to a path and climbs through open woodland to reach another path. Turn right through more lovely woodland (where wildflowers include ramsons and field mouse-ear). The path descends past a cottage onto a track running above the shore and underneath the fort of Mote of Mark.

6 **NX844540** Turn left and follow the track, with good views of Rough Island. Pass a house and go through a gate at a cattle grid. After the track swings left, turn right onto a path, which crosses a footbridge over a burn into a field. Follow this path along the field edge. Then go through a gate, turn left, descend through another gate down into Rockcliffe. Turn left and follow the pavement around the beach and climb Millbrae back to the car park.

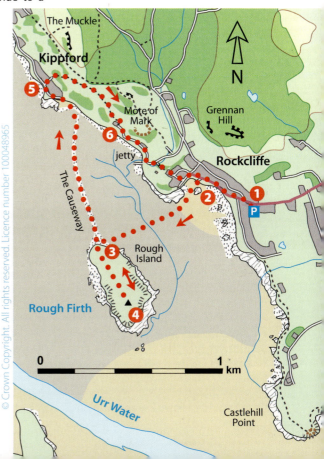

5

From the busy streets and historic buildings of Dumfries, many associated with Robert Burns, a peaceful walk along the River Nith leads to the quiet backwater of Kingholm Quay.

Dumfries & the River Nith

Start	Whitesands Car Park, Dumfries **NX970760**
Grade	■■□□□□
Distance	7.2km (4.5 miles)
Ascent	Negligible
Time	2 hours
Terrain	Pavement and riverside paths.

Getting there: The walk begins from the car park on Whitesands, opposite Dumfries Visitor Information Centre.
Public transport: There are good rail and bus links to Dumfries from Glasgow, Edinburgh and Carlisle.

This walk visits Robert Burns' landmarks that lie within Dumfries. The harbour at Kingholm Quay is a superb viewpoint.

1 **NX970760** Facing the River Nith, turn right and follow the pavement along Whitesands, passing the Devorgilla Bridge (named after Lady Devorgilla, mother of King John Balliol, who founded Balliol College in Oxford). The 15th century stone structure is one of many fine bridges spanning the Nith. At a set of traffic lights turn right onto Buccleuch Street (A780). Walk towards Greyfriars Kirk and, where the wonderful statue of Robert Burns stands on a traffic island, bear right into High Street.

ABOVE: *Devorgilla Bridge & the River Nith (point 1)*

OPPOSITE: *The River Nith from Dock Park (point 4)*

Dumfries has a rich and turbulent history. Its origins stretch back to 1186 when it was founded as a Royal Burgh, then grew swiftly as a market town and port. In 1306, Robert the Bruce killed John 'the Red' Comyn, his rival for the Scottish throne, in Dumfries. Bruce lured Comyn to Greyfriars Kirk and, when his request for Comyn's support was denied, he drew his dagger and killed Comyn beneath the High Altar. Bruce was excommunicated, but continued his campaign for Scottish independence and, seven weeks later, after more bloodshed, he was crowned King of Scotland.

Robert Burns is Scotland's greatest literary figure; his work is renowned across the globe with *Ae Fond Kiss* and *Auld Lang Syne* being two of his best-known works. Having moved to Ellisland (on the outskirts of Dumfries) in 1788, he wrote his most famous work, *Tam o' Shanter*. He then moved to Dumfries in 1791 and continued a productive period by writing over 100 songs for *Melodies of Scotland*. By 1795 Burns' was ailing and he died in Dumfries on the 21st July 1796 aged only 37. His remains are in the Burns Mausoleum in St Michael's Church graveyard.

2 **NX972763** Walk along the pedestrianised High Street passing Mid Steeple (built in 1707 to replace the Mercat Cross) and a conspicuous fountain. At an alleyway, signposted for the Globe Inn, turn left past what was Robert Burns' favourite inn. Walk along the narrow alley past the Burns Howff Club Millennium Time Capsule. Turn left then right and follow a ramp down to Shakespeare Street.

3 **NX973758** Cross the road, walk to the right then turn first left into Burns Street, where Robert Burns House is found. Burns moved here in 1793 from the Wee Vennel (now Bank Street) and died here on the 21st July 1796. Pass the house and keep left to the statue of Jean Armour (Burns' wife) by a set of traffic lights at Brooms Road (A756). Cross over to St Michael's Church and the Burns Mausoleum. Turn right, cross the B725 and descend St Michael's Bridge Road, past a public car park, to Dock Park.

4 **NX974756** Turn left into Dock Park and follow the tree-lined path above the River Nith, looking out for swans, ducks and herons. At the far end, turn right onto Kingholm Road (B726) and walk along the pavement past the Kirkpatrick MacMillan Bridge (Kirkpatrick MacMillan was born just north of Dumfries and is generally recognised as the inventor of the pedal bicycle).

5 **NX975747** Where the road leaves the riverside, bear right onto a path that leads through a small car park beside a cricket pitch. Continue above the Nith through parkland to reach the harbour at Kingholm Quay, which has lovely views of Criffel.

6 **NX975737** Retrace your steps back to the Kirkpatrick MacMillan Bridge, which was opened in 2006 as a key link in the National Cycle Network. Cross it to the other side of the River Nith.

7 **NX976749** Turn right and follow the riverside path past Troqueer Cemetery and old red sandstone mill buildings. Walk under the archways of St Michael's Bridge and

continue past the River Nith Suspension Bridge and the Robert Burns Centre. At Devorgilla Bridge, turn right back over the River Nith then go right to return to Whitesands car park.

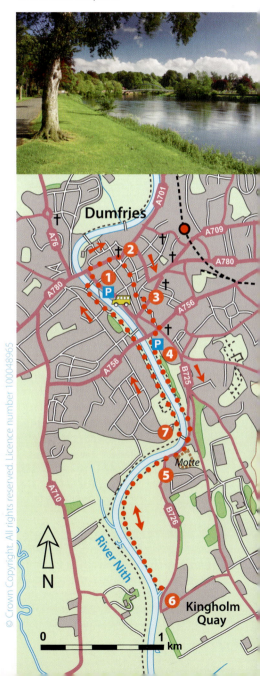

6

Dalbeattie Forest is a great place for wildlife; roe deer, bats, badgers and butterflies thrive in the wood, and you may spot a nuthatch or sparrowhawk.

Dalbeattie Forest

Start	Car park at Colvend Public Hall **NX868545**
Grade	☐☐☐☐☐
Distance	8km (5 miles)
Ascent	80m (260ft)
Time	2 to 2.5 hours
Terrain	Single-track road and forest tracks.

Getting there: Colvend is on the A710, 6 miles southeast of Dalbeattie and 20 miles southwest of Dumfries.

Public transport: Regular Stagecoach buses Service 372A from Dalbeattie to Colvend.

Dalbeattie Forest is one of the renowned, world-class, 7stanes mountain biking trail centres, which are located at seven sites across Southern Scotland. Much of this route utilises well-maintained forest tracks that are used by these trails.

❶ **NX868545** Facing Colvend Public Hall take a private road to the right and follow this towards Dalbeattie Forest, past several houses and through lovely mixed woodland. There are glimpses of White Loch to the left. Once past the last house, the track narrows to a path and climbs to a gate.

❷ **NX867549** Go through the gate and follow a broad stony track into Dalbeattie Forest, much of it recently replanted with a variety of native and mixed woodland. The track climbs gently then levels out and continues to attractive Barean Loch. There is a seat here if you wish to enjoy the view and

Dalbeattie Forest covers over 1000 hectares, stretching from Dalbeattie southwards for six miles to Colvend. The area was simply rough grazing and granite outcrops until planting of the forest began in the 1920s. Although the forest is dominated by Sitka spruce for harvesting, there are sections of native oak, ash, birch and Scots pine with more being planted. The forest contains a wonderful selection of wildflowers, including bluebells, wood anemones and red campion. Red squirrels do well here and it is a good place to see burnet moths and peacock butterflies.

Barean Loch sits just north of the village of Colvend and is a beautiful stretch of water, popular with fishermen. In 1865 a crannog (a type of ancient island structure that was used across Scotland and Ireland for loch-dwelling) was found here during drainage work. It consisted of a circle of oak piles enclosing a wood floor. Two bronze cooking pots, similar to Roman soldiers' cooking pots, were also uncovered.

the wildlife, which may include a heron. Pass a track on the right and walk along the banks of the loch, continuing uphill to a junction.

❸ **NX861559** Turn right at the junction and follow the track as it climbs steeply away from the loch. At the top of the climb, the track meanders through the forest (comprising a mixture of birch, Scots pine and spruce), past a track on the left, and comes to a junction.

❹ **NX869559** Turn left here and follow the main track beside Sitka spruce below

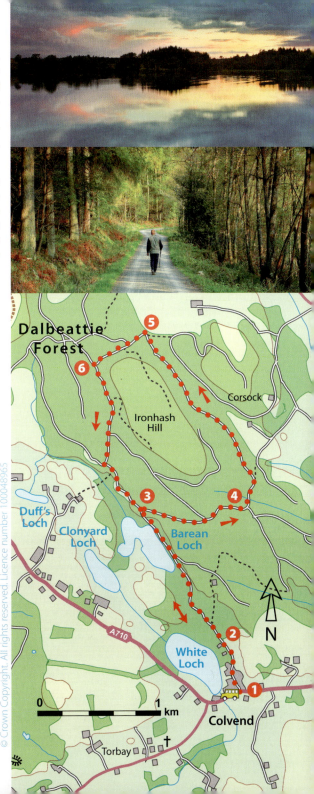

Ironhash Hill. As the track swings left, ignore a path to the right. There are several offshoot paths throughout the walk but keep to the main track. Spruce gives way again to more mixed woodland and after approximately 1.2km, you pass a path on the right, which leads to Corsock Farm.

5 **NX861574** Here keep to the main track as it swings left before passing some forest clearings, which offer great open views – the colours during autumn are outstanding. Pass a track on the right and continue to a T-Junction.

6 **NX855572** Turn left onto a track leading back into the trees. During spring and summer wood anemone, crowberry, bluebells and red campion line the verges – also lookout for adders sunning themselves. You are soon going downhill, with further great views appearing across Clonyard Loch. Ignore paths on the left and continue to a T-junction.

7 **NX857563** Turn left to head back towards Colvend, passing a path on the right, which is signposted for the A710. Walk beside some beautiful birch and rowan (again stunning in autumn) with wonderful views over open countryside to Screel and Bengairn. Continue along the track, which re-enters conifer forest and rejoins the outward track at **3**. Fork right and descend to the banks of Barean Loch. Follow the track back to the private road then carry on to reach Colvend.

ABOVE TOP: *Evening calm at Barean Loch (between points 2 and 3)*

ABOVE BOTTOM: *Autumn walk in Dalbeattie Forest (point 7)*

7

Only 15 miles of the Solway Firth separate Southerness from the Cumbrian coast, and the views towards the muscular Lake District mountains – particularly at dusk – are breathtaking.

Southerness & John Paul Jones

Start	Southerness Lighthouse **NX977543**
Grade	☐☐☐☐☐
Distance	11.2km (7 miles)
Ascent	55m (180ft)
Time	2 to 2.5 hours
Terrain	Beach, quiet country paths and roads.

Getting there: Southerness is off the A710, 16 miles south of Dumfries. There is a small car park just after the Paul Jones Hotel.
Public transport: Regular DGC bus service 372 from Dumfries to Southerness.

ABOVE: *John Paul Jones Cottage (point 5)*

Southerness is a village dominated by its lighthouse. The square-sided structure was built in 1749 as a marker to provide safe passage for ships entering the Nith estuary. A light was added in 1800. Southerness Golf Course is a superb 18-hole course that has often hosted the Scottish Boys and Scottish Amateur Championships. This area is internationally important for birds, with species such as sandpiper, greenshank and redshank taking advantage of the feeding possibilities at low tides. The Carboniferous rocks exposed on the shore are over 340 million years old and many fossils have been found over the years.

John Paul Jones is better known in the United States than in Scotland as he is considered to be the father of the American Navy. He was born on the estate of Arbigland, just a short distance from Southerness, on the 6th of July 1747. Aged 13, he boarded a vessel and sailed across the Solway to Whitehaven, where he signed up for a seaman apprenticeship. He was a captain of his own ship by the time he turned 21, and he eventually settled in North America becoming First Lieutenant in the Continental (later the United States) Navy in 1775. He died in Paris in 1792.

The first few miles from Southerness to Powillimount are along a lovely beach, but at very high tides parts of the route may be impassable. Therefore check tide times before starting (see page 10).

John Paul Jones Cottage is a small museum, where a visit is highly recommended. It is open 10am–5pm, Tuesday to Sunday from April to September and daily during July and August. There is a small admission charge.

❶ **NX977543** Facing Southerness Lighthouse, turn left and walk along the top of the stony beach, which has stunning views of Lake District. Walk past several cottages, some large sea defences and a caravan site. From here a wonderful, broad sandy beach stretches towards Powillimount and, if the tide is out, the sand is firm and great for walking along lower down the beach. Continue around the arc of sand and, immediately after the caravan park, cross a narrow burn, which may be problematic at high tides. The beach continues to a small car park at Powillimount.

2 NX989564 Here the beach becomes shingly. Pass the car park and follow a sandy path, which drops down onto a lovely secluded beach. Follow this beside woodland to reach the Thirl Stane Arch, a natural archway that has been pounded and shaped by the sea, and is popular with rock climbers.

3 NX993568 Retrace your steps to the car park and walk through it. Turn right onto a single-track road and follow it away from the coast with lovely views of Criffel. Walk through open countryside, passing Powillimount Farm and a cottage on the left. At a second cottage beside a strip of woodland, turn right onto a footpath signposted Carsethorn.

4 NX984567 Follow the woodland path, passing a small but very interesting cemetery containing graves of some of the Blackett family who used to own Arbigland Estate. Continue along a track to reach the entrance to John Paul Jones Cottage museum.

5 NX987571 Continue past the museum on a single-track road through trees. At a junction turn left away from Arbigland Estates on a woodland road to another junction.

6 NX984575 Go straight on here onto a quiet country road, which soon bends left, passing through lovely countryside with great views along the Colvend Coast. The road passes the access road to Powillimount then bends right past Maxwellfield Farm and runs between hedgerows, busy with greenfinch and chaffinch. The road then swings left to reach a junction.

7 NX971573 Turn left here onto a slightly busier road, heading towards Southerness. Pass East Preston and the scattering of houses at Loaningfoot, where the road bends left. The final mile back towards the lighthouse is past Southerness Golf Course.

BELOW: *Southerness Lighthouse at sunset (point 1)*

8

The Galloway coast looks delightful from the Waterloo Monument, which has a commanding view over the magnificent ruins of Sweetheart Abbey.

New Abbey & Waterloo Hill

Start	Sweetheart Abbey Car Park, New Abbey **NX965663**
Grade	■■■□□
Distance	4.4km (2.75 miles)
Ascent	180m (590ft)
Time	1.5 hours
Terrain	Quiet country roads with a steep hill path that climbs to the base of the Waterloo Monument.

Getting there: New Abbey is on the A710, 6 miles south of Dumfries.
Public transport: Regular DGC Bus Service 372 Dumfries to New Abbey.

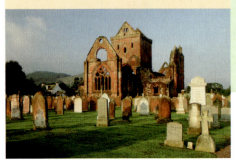

Sweetheart Abbey dominates New Abbey, the great sandstone edifice towering over the village. In 1273 Lady Devorgilla, one of the most powerful women of her time, decided to build it in memory of her late husband John Balliol who had died leaving her grief-stricken. She lavished funds on construction of the abbey, built of attractive red sandstone, and had Balliol's heart embalmed and placed in an ivory casket, which she kept with her when travelling. After her death in 1290 it was buried with her at the abbey, and the monks renamed the abbey Dulce Cor, Sweetheart Abbey. The roofless ruins are in the care of Historic Scotland and there is an entrance charge.

The Waterloo Monument provides a striking landmark above New Abbey. The 65-foot-high Grade B Listed Building was built in 1816 to commemorate the bravery of British, Belgian and Prussian soldiers in the Battle of Waterloo, which took place in Belgium a year earlier.

ABOVE: *Loch Kindar, Knockendoch and Criffel from the Waterloo Monument (point 4)*

LEFT: *The magnificent remains of Sweetheart Abbey (point 1)*

New Abbey is home to three popular visitor attractions – The National Museum of Costume, The New Abbey Cornmill and the stunning ruins of Sweetheart Abbey. The village is also the burial place of Sir William Paterson, founder of the Bank of England.

Return from Waterloo Hill (**4**) by the outward route or complete the circuit by continuing on a faint path over rougher ground, where trees have recently been clear felled.

❶ NX965663 From the car park walk past Sweetheart Abbey and turn right onto Main Street (A710). Walk along the narrow pavement to The Square. Turn left before reaching the Cornmill (a visit is highly recommended). Follow a road towards the millpond and turn left before it onto a minor road, signposted for the Waterloo Monument.

❷ NX962662 Follow this quiet, narrow road as it climbs gradually away from New Abbey through lovely countryside. As it swings sharply to the left, you get great views of both Criffel and Sweetheart Abbey. After the next bend, the Waterloo Monument is conspicuous, high above on the hillside. Wildflowers such as birdsfoot trefoil and red clover line the road, while yellow hammer, goldfinch and other birds sing in the hedges.

❸ NX956655 Leave the road where it swings left at a cottage and keep straight on, past the cottage, to join a track signposted for the monument. Go through a gate onto a path beside the Glen Burn, and walk through mixed woodland of oak, alder, sycamore, birch and beech. The path then begins to climb steeply. Beyond a gate, you emerge from

the woodland and the view opens out over the Nith Estuary, and southwards to nearby Loch Kindar and Criffel. Continue up the steep path (which can be overgrown), to the Waterloo Monument, where the panorama extends over New Abbey to the Galloway and Cumbrian coasts. It is possible to climb to the top of the monument via a very narrow, spiral staircase but extreme care should be taken if doing so. The top is very exposed.

❹ NX953656 The simplest return to New Abbey is by the route of ascent. Another interesting route follows a path that – due to recent tree felling – can be overgrown and, at points, rough underfoot. For the full circuit, walk past the monument and take the middle of three paths. Follow this in a north-westerly direction down the heathery hillside, carefully descending the path into a wood and down to a burn. Turn right and follow a good path beside the burn and through the wood to a farm track.

❺ NX952663 Turn right along the track, which develops into a single-track road. Pass some cottages, then a sawmill and the millpond and continue back to The Square. Turn right onto Main Street and walk through the village to return to Sweetheart Abbey.

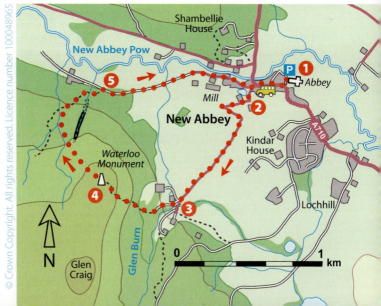

9

Standing at the edge of Scotland, you are struck by the seemingly endless expanse of water, only broken by distant views of the Isle of Man and Ireland.

Mull of Galloway

Start	Visitor Centre Car Park **NX155304**
Grade	■■■□□
Distance	5.2km (3.25 miles)
Ascent	100m (330ft)
Time	1.5 to 2 hours
Terrain	Single-track road and cliff top paths, which run above an unprotected drop.

Getting there: The Mull of Galloway lies at the southern tip of Scotland, 21 miles south of Stranraer via the A77 and A716 to Drummore then minor roads. **Public transport:** None to start. Regular King of Kirkcowan bus service 407 from Stranraer to Drummore, which is 4 miles from the start.

The Mull of Galloway is the peninsula at the southwest tip of Scotland. The southernmost point of the country is a rocky promontory a little west of the lighthouse – Gallie Craig – (also the name of an excellent coffee shop at the start of the walk). The coastline here is incredibly rugged with beautifully coloured cliffs rising steeply to over 250 feet (75m) and providing outstanding views.

The Mull of Galloway is an RSPB nature reserve with rich and diverse wildlife, ranging from tiny lichens to basking sharks. Puffin, fulmar, kittiwake, shag, razorbill and guillemot nest on the cliffs, while wall brown and grayling butterflies thrive in the warmer climate that the Gulf Stream provides. The visitor centre is in a whitewashed cottage near the lighthouse.

The Mull of Galloway Lighthouse was built by Robert Stevenson (one of the famous lighthouse building family), who also built nearby Corsewall Lighthouse. Work on the 26m-high cliff top structure was completed in 1830. The light is 99m (325 feet) above sea level and on a clear night can be seen from 28 miles away. It is open to the public at weekends from Easter to October, and on Mondays in July and August.

The cliff top paths provide an invigorating walk high above the sea. They run outside a fence, so there is no protection from the drop, and are exposed to the full force of wind and weather, so real care should be taken when walking them. Livestock graze the grassy plateau and aren't always fenced, and so it is advisable to keep dogs on leads.

❶ NX155304 From the car park, go through a gate and walk towards the lighthouse. Take the first path on the left and follow the grassy way across some heathery ground to the RSPB visitor centre. Beyond the building join a single-track road then turn left, crossing over a helicopter landing area, onto a path signposted for the foghorn. Bear right, to a wall, and pick up a path that leads to a flight of steep steps. Descend to the foghorn, which provides a superb vantage point, overlooking seabird colonies.

❷ NX157303 Retrace your steps then follow the path around the perimeter wall of the lighthouse compound to the entrance. Turn right onto a grassy path and follow it back to the car park. Descend to the Gallie Craig Coffee Shop, a modern, turf-roofed building.

❸ NX154304 Turn left and walk past the coffee shop. Go through a gate and turn right onto a grassy path to follow the exhilarating cliff top walk along the rugged coastline, keeping the fence to your right. The path runs very close to the cliff edge at times so be

careful. Continue for approximately 1.2km, passing Gallie Craig, before reaching a gate opposite the distinctive Kennedy's Cairn. Turn right through the gate and cross the field to the cairn, which rises impressively to over eight feet with steps leading to the top.

❹ NX146304 Retrace your steps back through the gate and continue along the cliffs towards West Tarbet bay. Beyond another gate, cross a short section of field above the bay to reach the road.

❺ NX143309 Walk to the right along the road for a few metres then turn left on a track down to East Tarbet. Go through a gate and walk to the right past an old cottage beside a slipway to pick up a faint path, which climbs steeply up a slope to a fence. Here the path levels out and continues beside the fence with steep slopes dropping down to the sea. Again it makes for spectacular walking, although the path can be rough underfoot at times. Continue along the Mull's undulating northern coast for around 1.5km to a wall that runs inland as you near the lighthouse.

❻ NX156307 Turn right through a gate and follow the wall, climbing steeply to another gate, which leads back into the car park.

OPPOSITE TOP: *View north from the Mull of Galloway Visitor Centre (between points 1 & 2)*

OPPOSITE BOTTTOM: *The Mull of Galloway Lighthouse at Scotland's southernmost tip (point 2)*

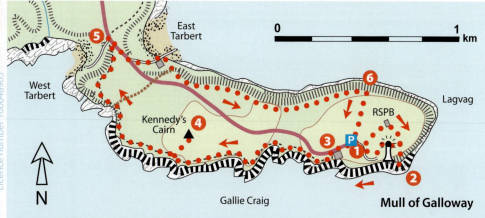

10

Although only 100m high, the view from The Muckle is remarkable, extending along the Colvend Coast to the mighty mountains of the Lake District.

Kippford & The Muckle

Start	Kippford Village Hall **NX836554**
Grade	■■■☐☐
Distance	4.8km (3 miles)
Ascent	140m (460ft)
Time	2 hours
Terrain	Pavement, single-track road, hill and woodland paths. Steep climbs onto The Muckle and Mote of Mark with wonderful views throughout.

Getting there: Kippford lies off the A710, 4 miles south of Dalbeattie and 18 miles southwest of Dumfries. Park at Village Hall.
Public transport: Regular DGC buses Service 372 from Dalbeattie to Kippford.

Most of this walk is on good paths and tracks, with a quiet, single-track road leading back into Kippford. Short but steep ascents and descents are required to reach both The Muckle and Mote of Mark.

Kippford commands a stunning position on the Urr estuary, where wading birds such as redshank and curlew dine on the rich pickings found within the mudbanks. Originally known as Scaur, the village developed around its harbour at the end of the 18th century. Over the next 100 years it became a sizeable port with small sloops being built on the shore and 350-400 tonne ships frequently visiting the pier. By the early 20th century, Kippford's significance as a port had declined and tourism began to take over. Today it is an important centre for yachting and a popular holiday destination.

Mote of Mark was a defended hilltop believed to be the court of a mighty Dark Age Chieftain, possibly a prince of Rheged, an ancient kingdom in northwest England. The site was certainly occupied during the 6th century but was destroyed by fire during the 7th. Excavations over the years have found the remains of a timber hut, imported jewellery, metalwork and glassware.

1 NX836554 From Kippford Village Hall cross the main road opposite Solway Yacht Club and turn left to walk along the pavement through the village. Beyond the RNLI Station and Kippford Slipway, turn left onto the Jubilee Path (named after Queen Victoria's Diamond Jubilee of 1901).

2 NX837549 Climb the single-track road, swinging right and passing houses, with great views over the coast, particularly towards Screel and Bengairn. Beyond the last house, the road narrows to a path and continues high above the coast through attractive woodland where woodpecker and red squirrel are common (on rare occasions nuthatch may be seen). Stay on the path until reaching a boulder with two arrows painted on it pointing to the left.

3 NX839545 Turn left here onto an obvious path, which climbs steeply through woodland to the summit of The Muckle. On a good day the views are breathtaking, extending along the Colvend Coast and across the Solway Firth to the Lake District.

4 NX841546 Retrace your steps back to the boulder and turn left along the Jubilee Path. Follow it for approximately half a mile (0.8km) to reach a signpost for the Mote of Mark, just before a single-track road.

5 NX846543 Turn right onto the path, going downhill and through a gate. Continue through a second gate and turn left. Just before another gate, turn right and climb a steep path to the summit of the Mote of Mark, which provides more wonderful views.

6 NX844540 Return to the main path, turn right through the gate and walk across an open field. Go over a bridge, bear right and walk across another field (where Highland cattle may be grazing). At the field edge, turn right onto a path and follow it to a footbridge. Cross over, turn left and continue along the path to a gate at a cattle grid.

7 NX845538 Once through the gate, follow a single-track road above the rocky shore, passing a house. At a cottage, bear right onto a path that soon bends left and climbs through mixed woodland. Follow the main path to a fork then go left and continue above the coastline, on a path lined with wildflowers. This path descends to a single-track road.

8 NX841542 Turn right and follow the road along the shore, past some large stone villas, into Kippford. Continue through the village back to the start.

OPPOSITE: *Kippford reflected in Rough Firth at dusk (point 1)*

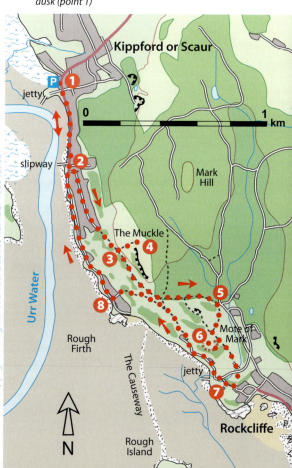

11

Step back in time as you stroll through ancient woodland to an imposing castle then climb a hill where sentinels watched the coast for approaching adversaries.

Caerlaverock Castle & Ward Law

Start	Caerlaverock Nature Reserve car park **NY019653**
Grade	☐☐☐☐☐
Distance	5.6km (3.5 miles)
Ascent	100m (315ft)
Time	2 hours
Terrain	Woodland and hill paths, tarmac lane.

Getting there: Take the B725 south from Dumfries for 8 miles; Caerlaverock Nature Reserve car park is on the right where the road bends left by a wood.
Public transport: Regular Stagecoach Bus Service 6A from Dumfries to Caerlaverock.

BELOW: *Criffel from Ward Law (point 5)*

OPPOSITE: *Caerlaverock Castle (point 3)*

This there-and-back walk follows an excellent path through Castle Wood to the picturesque remains of Caerlaverock Castle. Beyond, the route climbs onto the 96m high summit of Ward Law, which offers outstanding views of Criffel and the Solway Firth.

Caerlaverock Nature Reserve is a vast area of mudflats and saltmarsh, where the entire population of Svalbard barnacle geese spend their winter months, flying 2000 miles from the Arctic. Other winter visitors include whooper swan and many waders that feed on the exposed mudflats. In spring, ospreys arrive and the reserve starts to ring with the soaring song of skylarks and the noisy mating calls of natterjack toads. Summer warmth brings out butterflies and dragonflies, and carpets of wildflowers.

Caerlaverock Castle's history goes back to 1220 when a small castle was built by Sir John De Macusswell. It was replaced in 1270 by the striking, triangular structure – surrounded by a moat – that we see today. Caerlaverock's location near the Scottish–English border made it a focus for Edward I, the infamous 'Hammer of the Scots'. It survived various attacks until marauding Covenanters captured it in 1640 and demolished one wall. The ruins are in the care of Historic Scotland and are open all year. There is an entrance charge.

Castle Wood is a fine example of ancient semi-natural woodland containing alder, ash, hazel, birch and oak. Many of the trees are over 200 years old. The wood abounds in animals – including roe deer, otters, and badgers – and wildflowers such as ragged robin, orchids and holy grass, which is a rare coastal plant only found in Scotland and Ireland.

1 NY019653 From the car park, go around a gate onto a broad track leading towards Castle Wood. The track skirts the ancient woodland with the broad expanse of the saltmarsh and mudflats of the Solway Firth on the right. It then enters the wood and meanders between the wonderful old trees, crossing a bridge. At a bird watching hide the track bears left and crosses another two wooden footbridges before leading onto a broader track.

2 NY027654 Pass a couple of houses, continuing through Castle Wood to the site of the original Caerlaverock Castle, now surrounded by wet woodland. Here turn left onto a path, which runs past the castle foundations, then bears right down a flight of wooden steps and onto a boardwalk. Follow the boardwalk out of Castle Wood to the magnificent remains of Caerlaverock Castle.

3 NY025655 Walk around the grassy banks of the castle moat (to left or right of the castle) and onto a path leading up a grassy slope. Walk past the visitor centre and tearoom and onto the single-track entrance drive that swings right through an archway. Follow the lane, bending left to reach the B725.

4 NY026660 Cross straight over the road onto a farm track. At a fork, keep right to climb a grassy track towards Ward Law, its wooded summit high on the hillside ahead. The track follows a field boundary. Keep straight ahead through two gates (livestock may be grazing in the fields here) onto a fenced, grassy track that climbs steadily. At the top, go through a gate and immediately turn right through another onto a fenced path that climbs gradually to Ward Law. Cross a stile onto the atmospheric summit.

5 NY025666 Ward Law was the traditional meeting place and a watch station for Clan Maxwell in times of strife. With outstanding views along the coast, it would have been the perfect spot to observe the approach of any adversaries and warn clan members by lighting signal fires. From the summit retrace your steps back to Caerlaverock Castle, where a visit inside the castle is highly recommended; tickets can be bought from the visitor centre. Return via the outward route through Castle Wood to the start.

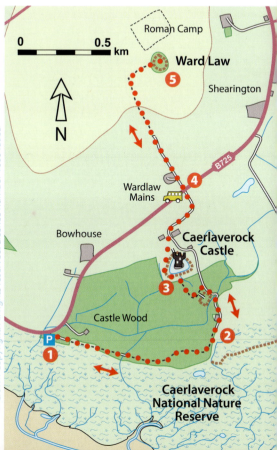

12

The clifftop paths, open countryside and lochside scenery along this route are testament to the beauty and diversity of the Galloway coast.

Balcary Bay & Loch Mackie

Start	Balcary Bay Hotel **NX821495**
Grade	■ ■ ■ □ □
Distance	6km (3.75 miles)
Ascent	70m (230ft)
Time	2.5 hours
Terrain	Paths, which can be exposed in places, above magnificent cliffs, quiet country paths and tracks with wonderful views throughout.

Getting there: Balcary Bay Hotel is at the end of a minor road, 1.5 miles southeast of the village of Auchencairn on the A711.
Public transport: Service 516 DGC Buses from Castle Douglas to Auchencairn then a pleasant 1.5-mile walk to the start.

Balcary Point is a spectacular location and a hive of activity as the steep cliffs are home to thriving colonies of kittiwakes, fulmars, guillemots and razorbills. At low tide, oystercatcher, dunlin, curlew and other waders frequently feed on the exposed shore. Paths are lined with wildflowers, including cushions of sea pinks, the conspicuous white sea campion and vibrant purple orchids. There is an appealing view of nearby Hestan Island and a wider panorama of the Galloway coast.

Hestan Island has had several residents, including the Reverend Beryl Scott, who detailed her experiences in her wonderful book *On a Galloway Island*. The author Samuel Rutherford Crockett used Hestan as the location for his novel *The Raiders*.

Loch Mackie is a sharp contrast to the lively surrounds of the cliffs between Balcary Point and Rascarrel Bay. It has a very peaceful location with wonderful views across open countryside to the twin peaks of Screel and Bengairn. The loch is ideal habitat for cormorant, mallard and goldeneye and is popular for fishing.

Starting at the welcoming Balcary Bay Hotel (a wonderful vantage point across Balcary Bay), this route uses excellent paths, although part of the walk is close to the sheer cliffs that characterise this rugged section of the Galloway coastline. Care should be taken at these points. The walk also crosses farmland so it is advisable to keep dogs on leads.

1 **NX821495** Facing the Balcary Bay Hotel, turn right and walk along a minor road to a gate that is on the right at a bend in the road. Go through and follow a track a short distance to another gate. Then bear left and walk along a field edge, following an indistinct track to reach two gates at the edge of a wood.

2 **NX825495** Take the left gate into attractive broadleaved woodland and follow a good path past some houses and a converted boathouse. Climb out of the wood, going through a gate to Balcary Point, which on clear days is a stunning vantage point for viewing the coast all the way to Southerness Point.

3 **NX828493** The excellent path then turns right away from Balcary Point and climbs high above the rugged coastline with good views to Big Airds Hill and Little Airds Hill, both of which have remnants of forts on their tops. The path sticks close to cliff edge here and care should be taken, particularly in windy conditions. Climb past the huge rock stack of Lot's Wife. The gradient then eases, providing a fantastic high-level cliff walk until you descend past Adam's Chair, another sea stack, then more steeply to reach Airds Point.

4 **NX821483** The grassy path levels out and runs above the shore. Near Rascarrel Bay it broadens into a rough track and descends to the stony shore. Continue underneath a steep embankment then fork right. Follow a path through bracken then turn right onto a grassy track.

5 **NX811483** Go right at another fork just before the conspicuous wooden houses at the eastern end of Rascarrel Bay and follow the track around them to wooded Rascarrel Moss. Go through a gate and along a broad track running parallel with the conifer wood. Beyond another gate reach the pleasant setting of Loch Mackie, where there are fine views inland.

6 **NX808488** Just before the loch go through a gate and turn right onto a track that follows a field edge (where there may be livestock grazing). Pass through two more gates. Once beyond a ruined cottage and a farmhouse, go through another two gates and descend a rough, single-track road across farmland to the Auchencairn to Balcary Bay road. Turn right and walk a short distance to the Balcary Bay Hotel car park.

OPPOSITE: *Balcary Bay and Hestan Island (point 3)*

Auchenfad

Auchencairn Bay

Hestan Island

Auchencairn House

Balcary Bay

Hotel

P **1**

Tower

Balcary Point

2

Racarrel Moss

Loch Mackie

Airds

Little Airds Hill

Balcary Hill

3

Lot's Wife

6

Big Airds Hill

5

4

Adam's Chair

Aird's Point

Rascarrel Bay

N

0   1 km

13

A superb clifftop walk leads to Dunskey Glen, where the beautiful broadleaved woodland has delightful spring flowers and wonderful autumn colours.

Portpatrick & Dunskey Glen

Start	Portpatrick Harbour **NW998542**
Grade	☐☐☐☐☐
Distance	8km (5 miles)
Ascent	150m (490ft)
Time	2 hours
Terrain	Good waymarked clifftop paths, woods and road.

Getting there: Portpatrick lies at the end of the A77, six miles southwest of Stranraer. There are car parks at the harbour and off South Crescent.

Public transport: Regular buses from a variety of providers run between Stranraer and Portpatrick.

Dunskey Gardens were created in the 19th century and have only recently been returned to their former glory, having fallen into disrepair. Today the restored glasshouses grow peaches, nectarines and grapes, and the gardens are resplendent with roses and rhododendrons. There is an entrance charge for the Walled Garden and adjoining it is a Tearoom, open 10am–5pm. Wildflowers, especially snowdrops and bluebells, carpet the woodland in spring. An honesty box encourages contribution to the upkeep of the woodland paths.

The Southern Upland Way begins (or ends, depending on the direction you walk) at Portpatrick. Opened in 1984, the route runs coast to coast for 212 miles between Portpatrick and Cocksburnpath on the North Sea. With over 80 hills that rise above 2000ft and much wild and remote terrain, it is a challenging and rewarding long distance walk.

The start of this walk to Port Kale follows the same route as Walk 17 (Portpatrick and Killantringan). Thereafter it leaves the Southern Upland Way and enters Dunskey Glen, where paths run through oak, sycamore and beech woodland to Dunskey Gardens and the adjacent Tearoom. The walk returns to Portpatrick by the same route as Walk 17.

1 NW998542 From the north side of Portpatrick Harbour climb the Southern Upland Way (SUW) steps, which zigzag steeply onto the cliffs above the village. Pass the Portpatrick Hotel and follow the path, which can be exposed at times, to an old radio station, passing on the seaward side of the buildings. Continue along the dramatic coastline to a flight of steps.

② **NW994544** At the top of the steps, turn left onto a narrow road and walk between Portpatrick Dunskey Golf Course and some impressive sea stacks. Pass a radio mast and keep straight ahead on an undulating path between golf course and shore. At beautiful Port Mora, the narrow path zigzags steeply down to the shore. Cross a stone bridge and walk across the lovely secluded beach.

③ **NW992552** At the end of the beach ignore a grassy path on the right and instead climb left up some steps, from where a path traverses the headland to sheltered Port Kale.

④ **NW991552** Turn right onto a grassy track, away from the beach, by two conspicuous white hexagonal buildings. The way forks almost immediately. Take the left path into Dunskey Glen, following it through woodland alongside Dunskey Burn. Cross a footbridge and continue beside Dunskey Burn. After a second footbridge, bear left onto a path that climbs steadily, following the course of a tributary and crossing two more bridges. The path bears sharp right and climbs to a fork, where you go left before re-crossing Dunskey Burn by a lovely stone bridge above a spectacular waterfall.

⑤ **NW997558** Continue straight on to a single-track road. Turn left and follow the road through more woodland to a T-Junction.

⑥ **NW998556** Turn right, as signposted for Dunskey Tearoom. Follow the single-track road through woodland and open country for about 1 mile to Dunskey Home Farm. Bear right past the farm, following the road towards Portpatrick. Soon come to a path on the left and follow it through woodland, parallel

to the B738, to a driveway. Turn left and continue to Dunskey Gardens and Tearoom.

⑦ **NX003560** Retrace your steps back to the single-track road just south of Dunskey Home Farm and turn left along it.

⑧ **NX005552** Just before the B738, fork right onto a minor road and follow it to a cottage. Bear left opposite the cottage onto another woodland path. Where it returns to the minor road turn left and walk a short distance to the A77.

⑨ **NX005548** Turn right onto the A77 then immediately right again onto Heugh Road. Walk along it to the Portpatrick Hotel, ignoring side streets. Turn left through the hotel car park onto the Southern Upland Way and descend the steps to return to the harbour.

OPPOSITE: *Port Mora and Port Kale (view to points 3 & 4)*

14

Climb through heathland to Rutherford's Monument, above Cardroness Castle, for marvellous views over Fleet Bay then visit the ruined church where Rutherford was minister.

Gatehouse of Fleet & Anwoth

Start	Gatehouse of Fleet car park **NX599562**
Grade	■■■□□
Distance	7.2km (4.5 miles)
Ascent	100m (330ft)
Time	2 hours
Terrain	Pavement, minor roads, woodland and hill paths, boggy in one section.

Getting there: Gatehouse of Fleet is just off the A75, 14 miles southwest of Castle Douglas and 18 miles southeast of Newton Stewart. The car park is on the High Street, just east of Fleet Bridge.

Public transport: Regular Stagecoach Bus Service 500 from Castle Douglas and Newton Stewart to Gatehouse.

Cardroness Castle, a magnificent tower house, was built in the 15th century by the McCullochs and commanded a strong position overlooking Fleet Bay. The family were involved in many local disagreements and eventually lost the castle to their bitter rival John Gordon in 1628. The castle is in the care of Historic Scotland and there is an entrance charge.

Samuel Rutherford was born in the Scottish Borders and became minister of Anwoth Kirk in 1627. Although popular with his parishioners, he was a controversial figure. He was banished to Aberdeen in 1636 for nonconformity to religious doctrines, but in 1638 became Professor of Divinity at St Andrew's College. However his political book of 1644, Lex Rex, got him into more trouble and he was charged with treason in 1660. He died in 1661 before he could be tried. The 55ft monument in his name was raised above Anwoth in 1842.

Gatehouse of Fleet was simply a staging post until 1760 when it began to develop into a thriving industrial town. By the late 18th century it had four cotton mills, a tannery, a brewery and a brass foundry, as well as a port welcoming about 150 ships every year. This heritage can be explored in the Mill on the Fleet visitor centre, opposite the car park.

The Rutherford Monument and adjacent Trusty's Hill (an Iron Age fort with a Pictish carved stone) are high points amid a scattering of knolls surrounded by gorse and bracken. The paths are indistinct in places, so careful navigation is needed. Local wildlife includes roe deer, red kite and kestrel.

❶ NX599562 From the car park, turn left onto High Street and cross Fleet Bridge onto Fleet Street. Follow the pavement out of the village above the wooded banks of the River Fleet to Cardroness Castle.

❷ NX591552 Return towards the village but just before entering Gatehouse turn left into a residential road with a footpath sign for Anwoth. The road swings left and climbs quite steeply. Go right at a fork then turn left off the road through a gate signposted for a private garden (it is fine to do so).

❸ NX593562 Follow a narrow woodland path to stone steps crossing a wall. Then go through a gate and climb a steep path meandering through peaceful heathland. At an old stone wall the path dips downhill to a signpost, where you go straight on for Trusty's Hill. The path bears left, traversing the lower slopes, then bends right and climbs steeply. Pass a stone with the only known Pictish carving in southwest Scotland and gain the top of Trusty's Hill. Enjoy lovely views over Gatehouse of Fleet and to the Samuel Rutherford monument.

❹ NX589560 Continue across the hilltop on an indistinct path then drop down onto a more obvious path. It swings left and drops steeply to the wall, where a lower section is easy to cross. The path bends left again to cross a short section of very boggy ground. Once over this, follow a broad track up a field, where there may be livestock grazing. At the top of a hill turn left onto a path. A short descent then re-ascent brings you to the Samuel Rutherford monument and some wonderful views over Wigtown Bay to the Isle of Man.

❺ NX587557 Return to the track and go straight across it. Follow a path past a memorial that lists the ministers of Anwoth Church to a trig point.

❻ NX586559 Continue straight past the trig point down a grassy path to a T-junction. Turn left into a wood on a path that goes steeply downhill to a gate. Go through, cross a field path and then a bridge. Beyond another gate follow a track into Anwoth.

❼ NX583561 Turn right onto a minor road and pass the Old Schoolhouse (now a cottage) and the remains of Anwoth Old Kirk. Follow the road to the B796. Turn right and return along the quiet road into Gatehouse of Fleet, turning left across Fleet Bridge.

OPPOSITE TOP: *View to the Rutherford Monument (point 5) from Trusty's Hill (point 4)*

OPPOSITE BOTTOM: *Anwoth Kirk (point 7)*

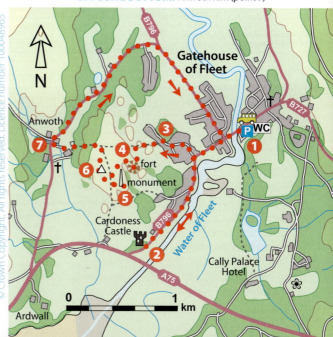

15

Waves crashing into Auchenmalg Bay are the only sound to break the over-riding sense of peace and quiet that permeates this isolated section of the lonely Machars coastline.

Auchenmalg & Stairhaven

Start	Luce Bay Caravan Park entrance **NX237517**
Grade	☐☐☐☐☐
Distance	9.6 km (6 miles)
Ascent	170m (550ft)
Time	2.5 hours
Terrain	Clifftop paths with several stiles, returning by minor roads.

Stairhaven is a scattering of houses on the shores of Luce Bay, plus a picnic site that has a superb view of the Rhins of Galloway. According to the Rev. C H Dick, in his book *Highways & Byways in Galloway and Carrick*, its derivation is 'a haven built by the Earl of Stair'. Dick also records that it used to be called The Craw's Nest, a corruption of Crossness, "the headland of the cross"– a reflection of The Machars close connections with early Christianity in Scotland.

Luce Bay is about 20 miles wide and is enclosed by the Rhinns of Galloway on the west and The Machars on the east. It is a Special Area of Conservation with a rich seabed, home to lobsters and sea anemones, and shores that are important feeding areas for many wintering wildfowl and waders. The dune system contains flower rich grassland and pools where great-crested newt breed. Visible a few kilometers south into Luce Bay are Little Scares and Big Scares, rocky islands that are home to 2000 breeding pairs of gannets as well as shags, kittiwakes and guillemots.

Getting there: Auchenmalg is on the A747, 4.5 miles southeast of Glenluce. There is a small amount of parking beside Auchenmalg Bay on The Barracks lane at **NX234518** (point **2**).
Public transport: Limited AF Irvine Bus Service 416 from Stranraer to Auchenmalg.

The **clifftop** route has some steep climbs and is waymarked throughout, which is helpful where paths are less distinct. Local signs request that dogs are not walked along the route as livestock graze on some sections.

1 **NX237517** Facing the caravan park turn left and walk along the A747 passing The Cock Inn. Walk uphill then turn left onto a minor road towards 'The Barracks'. Cross a bridge then turn left onto a track, again signposted for 'The Barracks', and follow it to the shore (if coming by car, start from here).

2 **NX234518** The track sweeps right along the shore then right again towards a house. As it rises, turn left onto a signposted path and climb steeply between gorse bushes to a fence.

3 NX231519 Go left along the clifftop coastal path, lined by sea pinks during spring and summer. Traverse the slopes of the Mull of Sinniness on the undulating path. Go over a stile then bear left, down a short, steep slope to a drystone wall. The path drops steeply left again, crosses a burn by some stepping-stones, and climbs a steep embankment. Continue, with wonderful views of the Isle of Man, then cross a second stile and descend a boggy section to another burn.

4 NX217522 Cross the burn, turn left and follow the edge of an open field (where livestock may be grazing) above the coast. Beyond a stile continue along a field-edge, looking out for the waymarked posts as the path peters out for a short distance. Once back on the path, climb to a waymarked post and drop left to another stile. Cross over and follow a grassy path over a further stile with marvellous views to the Rhinns of Galloway. Two more stiles are crossed, as the path climbs towards Stairhaven, before dropping steeply to a wall. Turn right then left and

continue steeply down, crossing a final stile into Stairhaven.

5 NX209537 Stairhaven is a lovely spot with a long, pebbly beach, overlooked by a car park and picnic site. Unless you want to visit these, turn immediately right onto the single-track road. Follow it away from the coast through fine countryside, passing a couple of cottages.

6 NX215543 Turn right at South Milton Farm onto a minor road and continue through the open Machars countryside. Pass a road on the right for Castle Sinniness and keep straight on, eventually dropping down into Auchenmalg. Pass Long Forth Farm and continue to 'The Barracks' track.

7 NX234522 If you parked by the shore, turn right here and follow the track back. If taking the bus, continue to the A747, turn right and return to Luce Bay Caravan Park.

OPPOSITE: *Stormy seas at Auchenmalg (Point 3)*

LEFT: *Fulmar gliding on the updraft from the cliffs*

16 Garlieston & Cruggleton Castle

This east facing coast, warmed by the Gulf Stream but sheltered from westerly gales, is home to lush gardens and rich wildlife, including curlew, dunlin, heron and grey seals.

Start	South Crescent, Garlieston **NX477463**
Grade	☐☐☐☐☐
Distance	11.2km (7 miles)
Ascent	40m (130ft)
Time	3 hours
Terrain	Coastal paths, through woodland, fields and along clifftops.

Getting there: Garlieston is 14 miles south of Newton Stewart, via the A714 to Wigton then the A746 and B7004. There is small car park at the start and some street parking within the village.
Public transport: Regular King of Kirkowan Bus Service 415 Newton Stewart to Garlieston.

Lovely coastal paths rise up to ruined Cruggleton Castle, where superb views along The Machars await. The walk then returns past the impressive Galloway House (once home to the Earls of Galloway) and through the lovely gardens.

Garlieston was named after Lord Garlies (the 7th Earl of Galloway) who built a small port here in the late 18th century. As a result, Garlieston's population expanded to 500 with sailcloth production and shipbuilding flourishing. Tourism also benefited with steamers regularly leaving from Garlieston for the Isle of Man. Between 1941 and 1944 Garlieston Bay was used to test components of the Mulberry floating harbours that were critical to the success of the D-Day landings in 1944.

Galloway House Gardens occupy a unique, sheltered position on Wigtown Bay. Dating back to 1740, they are set in over 50 acres of designed parkland. They are open to visitors all year and donations to the Trust that maintains them are very welcome.

Cruggleton Castle is a shadow of its former self but in its heyday would have been an impressive sight, as it had no fewer than eight towers. Edward I captured it during the first War of Independence (1296-1328), only for it to be retaken by Scotland's most famous patriot and freedom fighter, William Wallace.

1 **NX477463** Facing the harbour on South Crescent walk right, along the pavement past the village hall. Swing left past a caravan site, crossing a burn, and pass Garlieston Harbour.

2 **NX481462** Bear right onto a track, signposted for Rigg Bay. Walk above the shore, past a house and through a gate. Continue along a path above sea defences then fork right through a gate and keep on through fine woodland. Beyond another gate, fork left down to Rigg Bay, where a good path runs above the arc of the beach, passing a gate on the right that allows pedestrian access into Galloway Gardens.

3 **NX477449** The path bears left onto Rigg Bay. Make your way across the beach to reach an obvious track on the right. Follow this track a short distance to an old cottage.

4 **NX475446** Turn left onto a path over a stone footbridge and continue around Rigg Bay, through some magnificent beech woodland and over several wooden bridges, towards Sliddery Point.

5 **NX486440** The woodland path then climbs gently above the coast, past some wonderful old, gnarled trees to a house, where it goes through a stone doorway. Follow a clifftop path alongside a wall to a gate. Go through then keep left along a field edge, passing through two more gates. At Cruggleton Point, go left over a stile to reach the remains of Cruggleton Castle, where there are amazing views over the Isle of Whithorn to the Isle of Man. There are steep drops down to the shore so take care here.

6 **NX485428** Return via Sliddery Point to the old cottage at Rigg Bay (point **4**).

7 **NX475446** Turn left after the cottage onto a grassy track signposted 'woodland walk'. Follow it ignoring side paths. Turn right at a T-junction and continue along the track then turn right just before a gate. The track narrows to a path and crosses a wooden bridge, where it swings sharply left. Cross several more wooden bridges to reach another track. Turn left and continue through a gate onto a single-track road beside a walled garden. Walk past the walled garden, swinging left by two white gateposts. Turn right into Galloway House car park.

8 **NX477452** From the car park, turn left onto a path signposted for 'woodland garden'. This heads towards Galloway House, swinging right then turning left onto a track. Follow this past Galloway House to a fork and go left, signposted for 'The Pond'. Turn left at a crossroads and continue back to Rigg Bay. Return by the outward route to Garlieston.

OPPOSITE: *Garlieston seafront (point 1)*

17

Walk along the start of the Southern Upland Way, on an exhilarating clifftop path above seabird colonies, then return through woods full of wildflowers.

Portpatrick & Killantringan Bay

Start	Portpatrick Harbour **NW998542**
Grade	■ ■ ■ ☐ ☐
Distance	10km (6.25 miles)
Ascent	190m (620ft)
Time	3 hours
Terrain	Excellent waymarked clifftop paths then country roads and woodland paths.

Getting there: Portpatrick lies at the end of the A77, 6 miles south-west of Stranraer. There are car parks at the harbour and just off South Crescent.
Public transport: Regular buses from a variety of providers run between Stranraer and Portpatrick.

Portpatrick is a bustling, vibrant village built around an attractive working harbour. Its peaceful setting is appealing to walkers as well as tourists, as it is the start of the 212-mile Southern Upland Way. In the 1700s, Portpatrick was the main port for landing cattle from Ireland, which were then driven to market in Dumfries. In the early 19th century, there were regular sailings to Ireland, as well as the Isle of Man. However by the 1860s, Stranraer was the area's main port and Portpatrick then grew into a popular holiday resort.

Killantringan Lighthouse commands a dramatic position above Portamaggie. It was completed in 1900 and automated in 1988. Despite its warning beam, the 800-ton 'Craigantlet' ran aground here with its cargo of hazardous chemicals in 1982.

Walk past secluded coves at Port Mora and Port Kale to a spectacular beach at Killantringan Bay, with views to the Mull of Galloway and Northern Ireland. See Walk 13 for details of Dunskey Gardens and Tearoom.

❶ NW998542 From the north side of Portpatrick Harbour, climb the Southern Upland Way (SUW) steps, which zigzag steeply onto the cliffs above the village. Pass

the Portpatrick Hotel and follow the path to an old radio station, passing on the seaward side of the buildings. Continue along the dramatic coastline to a flight of steps.

❷ NW994544 At the top of the steps, turn left onto a narrow road and walk between Portpatrick Dunskey Golf Course and some impressive sea stacks. Pass a radio mast and keep straight ahead on an undulating path between golf course and shore. At beautiful Port Mora, the narrow path zigzags steeply down to the shore. Cross a stone bridge and walk across the lovely secluded beach.

3 NW992552 At the end of the beach ignore a grassy path on the right and instead climb left up some steps, from where a level path traverses the headland to sheltered Port Kale. Pass two conspicuous white hexagonal stone buildings, cross a wooden bridge and continue along the top of the beach. Join a stony path around some crags and climb two flights of steep steps.

4 NW989553 Head left over a stile and follow a grassy path across moorland for 1.5km (1 mile). At Portavaddie, descend steeply through a gate and follow a wall, going through it at a SUW sign. Cross a wooden bridge, go through a gate and keep right. Follow the path towards Killantringan Lighthouse, going through another gate and climbing a steep slope. Then descend towards Portamaggie, turning right onto a track behind the beach and following it up to a gate.

5 NW983566 Turn right onto a single-track road, passing a small car park and walking above breathtaking Killantringan Bay. The road (still the SUW) gradually climbs inland for 1.5 miles (2.5km) through farmland.

6 NW999575 At the B738, turn right (leaving the SUW) and follow the quiet road for 1.5km (1 mile), to the entrance to Dunskey Gardens.

7 NX006557 Turn right into the driveway, go 20m then turn left onto

a signposted footpath (keep straight on for the tearoom). Meander through peaceful woodland to a single-track road just south of Dunskey Home Farm. Turn left towards the B738.

8 NX005552 Just before the B738, fork right onto a minor road and follow it to a cottage. Bear left opposite the cottage onto another woodland path. Where it returns to the minor road turn left and walk a short distance to the A77.

9 NX005548 Turn right then immediately right again into Heugh Road. Walk along it to the Portpatrick Hotel, ignoring side streets. Turn left through the hotel car park onto the Southern Upland Way and descend the steps to return to the harbour.

OPPOSITE TOP: *Portpatrick harbour (point 1)*
OPPOSITE BOTTOM: *View to Killantringan Lighthouse (from near point 5)*

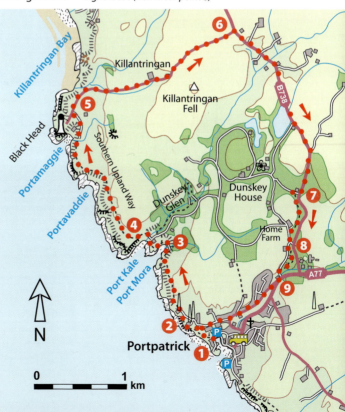

18
A long but easy circuit that explores a wonderful array of habitats, from river, wood and rolling pasture to sandy beaches and island-studded rocky shore.

Sandgreen & Carrick Shore

Start	Gatehouse of Fleet car park **NX599562**
Grade	■■■□□
Distance	19.2km (12 miles) or 14.4km (9 miles)
Ascent	140m (450ft)
Time	5 or 4 hours
Terrain	Woodland paths and tracks, single-track roads and beach.

Getting there: Gatehouse of Fleet is just off the A75, 14 miles southwest of Castle Douglas and 18 miles southeast of Newton Stewart. The car park is on the High Street, just east of Fleet Bridge. **Public transport:** Regular Stagecoach Bus Service 500 from Castle Douglas and Newton Stewart to Gatehouse.

RIGHT: *The beach at Sandgreen (Point 4)*

OPPOSITE: *Shell at Sandgreen*

Cally House is a breathtaking A-Listed building (now a hotel) that was built in 1763 for James Murray of Broughton. Less distinguished, but equally significant, is Lady Ann Murray's Charity School, established in the early 19th century for girls aged between 3 and 14. The Gatehouse Initiative, in conjunction with the Forestry Commission, is in the process of rebuilding the historic school.

Garries Wood, Cally Park and Cally Mains Wood are mixed woodland of oak, beech, sycamore and birch that display a kaleidoscope of colour in autumn. Home to red squirrel and roe deer, they contain a wealth of birdlife, including buzzard, woodpecker, spotted flycatcher, tree creeper and kingfisher. In spring the woodland is carpeted with bluebells, ramsons and other wildflowers.

The Islands of Fleet – Murray's Isles, Ardwall Isle and Barlocco Isle – lie at the mouth of Fleet Bay. Murray's Isles are owned by the National Trust for Scotland and contain regionally important colonies of gulls and cormorants. Excavations have found Norse graves on Ardwall Isle, and during the 17th and 18th centuries it was used by smugglers for hiding contraband.

This relatively flat walk is fairly easy to navigate. A shortcut between points **5** and **8** can reduce the distance by 5km (3 miles). The full route passes Rainton Farm, home of luxury ice cream maker Cream o' Galloway (visitor centre open February to November).

❶ **NX599562** Go through a gate beside the public toilets into Garries Wood. Follow a woodland track to a playing field, bear right around the field then back into the trees. Go straight across a junction onto a woodland path beside a river. Swing right over a bridge and continue to Cally Old School.

2 **NX599557** Turn left and follow a track through woodland, until it turns right over a bridge to a junction. Fork right onto a single-track road and pass several cottages.

3 **NX604554** Turn right onto the driveway to Cally Palace, walking beside a golf course. Beyond the hotel, descend into woodland and pass under the A75. Follow the single-track road to Cally Mains Farm. Here you fork right past the farm then rejoin the road, ignoring a track to the right. Continue through woodland, forking right as signposted for Sandgreen. Leave the wood by a gate and keep ahead on a track that descends through scenic countryside.

4 **NX577526** At Sandgreen Caravan Park, fork right then join the road through the park. As it swings right, keep straight ahead on a sandy path. Turn left along a lovely beach, leaving it by a grassy track onto a single-track road. Follow the straight road past fields to a junction beside a cottage.

5 **NX581515** Turn right (or left for a shortcut to **8**) onto a rougher road that meanders along the coast, past some wooden cottages. Fork right for Carrick Bay, where there are superb views of Murray's Isles.

6 **NX577506** Follow a track that bends left alongside the beach then turn right on a road that continues along the coastline. Pass through a gate and go through a small car park beside a fine beach overlooking Ardwall Isle. Continue with good views of Barlocco Isle. Beyond a gate, the road veers away from the coast past Knockbrex Castle to a junction.

7 **NX587499** Turn left along a quiet country road for 2km (1.25

miles) until just before Lennox Plunton. Turn left, signposted Sandgreen, and continue through lovely countryside past Cream o' Galloway, or pause here for refreshments.

8 **NX597525** At the next junction, turn right. Beyond Girthon and before the A75, look out for a National Cycle Route 7 sign.

9 **NX609541** Turn left through a gate onto the signed cycle path. Cross two bridges and return into Cally Park woodland. Turn left at a junction, cross a bridge then turn right at the next junction. Walk through the woodland to the outward track. Turn right under the A75 and retrace your steps back to Gatehouse.

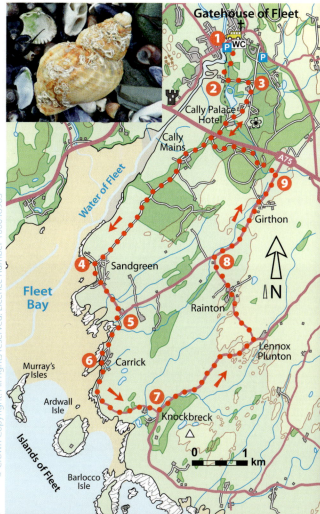

19
Screel

Screel may not be very high, but it is one of southern Scotland's finest vantage points, reached by a tough climb through woodland and up a steep, craggy hillside.

Start	Screel forest car park **NX800547**
Grade	☐☐☐☐☐
Distance	6km (3.75 miles)
Ascent	350m (1150ft)
Time	2.5 hours
Terrain	Forest roads and hill paths over craggy and heathery terrain with steep slopes and crags.

Getting there: Take the A711 southwest from Dalbeattie for 6 miles then, 2 miles north of Auchencairn, turn right, signposted Gelston. The car park is on the left, up a forest road.
Public transport: Regular ABC Travel Bus Service 505 Dalbeattie to Auchencairn.

Screel (343m) and the neighbouring hill of Bengairn are a conspicuous sight, rising to over 1000 feet above the Colvend Coast. Well used paths climb to Screel's broad summit for a truly astonishing panorama. The plains around Loch Ken draw the eye north to the Rhinns of Kells, while the view over Balcary Point and Hestan Island leads across the Solway Firth to the Lake District. The birdlife includes red kite, buzzard, kestrel, raven, grouse and goldcrest.

Smuggling was big business along the Galloway Coast during the 18th and 19th centuries, particularly around the coves and caves in this area. Sometimes entire villages were involved in this illegal practice. Tobacco, tea and silk were smuggled in from the Isle of Man, where customs duties were much lower than in Scotland. Custom officers watched the coast from vantage points, but were often bribed or turned a blind eye.

ABOVE: *Looking across the Colvend Coast from beneath the summit of Screel (point 4)*

Most of this walk is on distinct paths and tracks, but the route to the summit is less obvious in places. Much of the forestry beneath Screel has been clear felled and – at the time of writing – a short, awkward section of rough ground and dead branches has to be crossed on the way down. If you wish to avoid this, return by the route of ascent.

1 **NX800547** From the car park go around a barrier and walk up the forestry track, which swings right and climbs gradually through conifer forest to reach a junction.

2 **NX796546** Take the left fork, which leads towards a gate, but before reaching it turn right onto a path. Follow it steeply away from the track and through a section of open hillside to a seat beside a forest road.

3 **NX794547** Go straight across the forest road and continue on a path through conifer forest. Initially, the path climbs gently through the trees, but keep a close eye on its line, as it can be indistinct. After a couple of steeper sections, you emerge from the forest onto open hillside with the wonderful craggy profile of Screel ahead.

4 **NX788549** Follow the path as it climbs steeply, passing a seat from where magnificent views of the Galloway Coastline begin to open out. Beyond this, another steepish climb leads to more a level path, although this can be boggy at times. The path runs along a steep slope, which drops away to the left, with rock outcrops rising steeply above on the right. Keep on until the path swings right and climbs steeply, zigzagging through some crags onto Screel's broad ridge, where there are outstanding views of the Colvend Coast and Cumbria.

5 **NX785551** Turn left along the ridge and follow the undulating path northwest over heathery slopes to the large cairn on Screel's summit. Again, there are exceptional views of Galloway's coast and countryside. Return either by retracing your steps or by following the full route below.

6 **NX779553** The path descends west quite steeply to a wall. Follow it to the wall corner then head left to a rough track. Carefully make your way left along this track, a short section of which is covered in old branches. The track quickly improves and descends gently to a forest road, beside Glen of Screel Burn.

7 **NX783551** Turn left onto the forest road and follow it downhill, underneath Screel's long ridge and back towards the coast. Lower down, the road runs alongside a conifer forest then swings left to reach the seat beside the outward path (at point **3**).

8 **NX794547** Turn right and descend the path. On reaching the forest road you originally came up, turn right and follow it back to the car park.

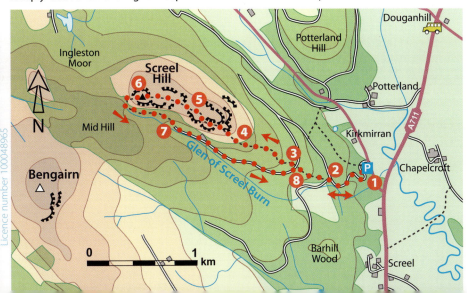

Licence number 100048965

20

This part of the Borgue Coast has a wild and remote feel, with a narrow clifftop path to ancient fortifications giving outstanding views along the Galloway coastline.

Brighouse Bay & Borness Fort

Start	Brighouse Bay car park **NX635458**
Grade	☐☐☐☐☐
Distance	7.2km (4.5 miles)
Ascent	80m (260ft)
Time	3 to 3.5 hours
Terrain	Woodland, field and coastal paths, rocky in one section, and single-track road.

Getting there: Brighouse Bay is 6 miles southwest of Kirkcudbright, via the A755, B727 and a minor road.

Public transport: None to start. Limited Stagecoach Bus Service 517 Kirkcudbright to Brighouse Bay Road end, 1.5 miles walk from the start.

BELOW: *View northwest to the Cairnsmore Hills from near Borness Batteries (point 5)*

The route is waymarked and generally on clear, grassy paths, but at Dunrod Point you cross an area of rocky pathless ground where the going is tough. During high tides this section may be problematic, especially if the sea is rough, so check tide times (see page 10).

Brighouse Bay is a lovely stretch of sand, hemmed in on both sides by a serrated coastline. The shore here is a Site of Special Scientific Interest and is the only place in Scotland where perennial flax is found. This lovely pale blue flower is rare in Britain, with most colonies found on dry, calcareous grassland on the east coast of England. The plant is vulnerable to camping, fires, overgrazing or encroaching scrub. It thrives here because southwesterly gales have driven sand onshore, enriching the soil with calcium carbonate.

Borness Batteries is a well-preserved prehistoric fort, strategically sited on a promontory. Earth banks and ditches defend it on the landward side. In a prehistoric cave dwelling nearby, excavations found 3586 bones of oxen, sheep, pigs, red deer, mice and 123 objects of human art in bone, stone, bronze, iron, and glass.

Cairniehill Loch has silted up to form a wetland with reeds, bulrushes and yellow irises. It provides an important pocket of habitat – amid the vast, rolling pastures – for newts, dragonflies and insect-eating birds, such as swallows and grey wagtails.

1 NX635458 Facing the public toilets, walk left to the end of the car park and follow a short road down to Brighouse Bay. Go around a wooden barrier onto a good path and follow it into lovely, mixed woodland, soon bearing right away from the shore.

2 NX632456 Just before the entrance to Brighouse Bay Caravan Park, turn left onto a wide path, which runs through the wood, parallel to the shore. Go left at a fork and continue through woodland, crossing a bridge. Turn left at a fence and follow the path out of the trees at a slipway.

3 NX631451 Join a track here and, as it swings right, bear left onto a grassy path through further woodland. Turn left at a fork and exit the woodland onto a rougher section of coastline. From here to Dunrod Point is rocky and hands may be required. It is best to keep to the top of the beach and care should be taken throughout.

4 NX627445 From Dunrod Point a good, grassy path leads to a fence by Brighouse Bay Golf Course. Follow it alongside an old lichen covered wall, which hugs the rugged coastline, weaving around its rocky indentations. The path climbs to the earthworks of Borness Batteries, which commands a fantastic view along the jagged coastline and inland to Cairnsmore of Fleet.

5 NX620447 Round the next cove then go through a gate and over a stile into a field. Take a grassy path heading inland between a fence and wall, with a golf course on the right. Go through a gap in the wall and continue uphill beside it. Pass through two gates before climbing to a cairn on Borness Bar.

6 NX621454 From here, you can see across Wigtown Bay to Burrow Head. Keep ahead on the path, descending across the field to a gate. Once through, continue down to a grassy track and go left along it to a track. (For a shortcut back to the start, turn right here and follow the track past Southpark Farm.)

7 NX622458 Go through a gate and straight across the track onto a waymarked grassy path. Follow it past a small pond and a cottage then beside the wetlands of Cairniehill Loch. The path crosses a grassy farm track and runs underneath Cairniehill.

8 NX626471 Go through a gate and turn right onto a track signposted for Brighouse Bay. Follow it through Cairniehill Farm and onto a single-track road towards the beach. Just before the main road, turn right through a waymarked gate onto a path across a field. Beyond another gate, go over the road and back into the car park.

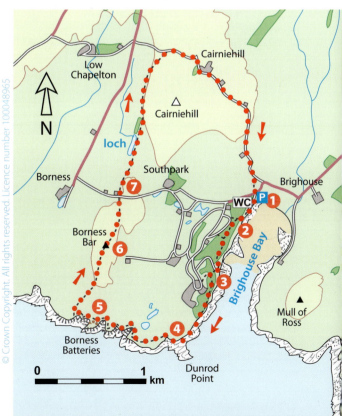

21

This linear route is one of Galloway's most spectacular walks, running past coves sheltered by woodland then along clifftops with stunning views and superb wildlife.

Kippford to Sandyhills

Start	Kippford Village Hall **NX836554**
Finish	Sandyhills **NX891553**
Grade	☐☐☐☐☐
Distance	9.6km (6 miles)
Ascent	275m (900ft)
Time	4 hours
Terrain	Woodland and cliff paths, exposed in places and with some steep climbs, and minor roads.

Getting there: Kippford lies off the A710, 4 miles south of Dalbeattie and 18 miles southwest of Dumfries. Park at the village hall.

Public transport: Regular DGC bus Service 372 from Dalbeattie to Kippford. Four 372A buses daily Monday to Friday from Sandyhills to Kippford, but only one on Saturday and none on Sunday.

The Colvend Coast runs for six miles between Kippford and Sandyhills, and hosts an exceptional range of flora and fauna. Roe deer, red squirrel, and sparrowhawk frequent the woods, peregrine falcon, fulmar and razorbill can be seen along the rocky coast, and wildflowers include bluebells, English stonecrop and orchids. The wildlife, beautiful scenery and outstanding views make this the jewel in Galloway's crown.

Solway Firth – the walk gives sweeping views over Mersehead Sands, a broad area of tidal flats traditionally used for cockle picking and salmon netting.

Castlehill Point is a small hill near Rockcliffe and the site of an Iron Age fort dating from 200AD. Some of the original ditches and stonework are still visible. Commanding views to the south and east would have made it an important defensive site.

OPPOSITE: *Looking over Portling from The Torrs (point 8)*

Between Castlehill Point and Sandyhills this stunning walk goes close to the exposed cliffs and has some stiff climbs. Keep an eye on return bus times as the service is limited, or park at Sandyhills and take the bus journey first.

❶ **NX836554** From Kippford Village Hall cross the main road opposite Solway Yacht Club and turn left to walk along the pavement through the village. Beyond the RNLI Station and Kippford Slipway, turn left onto the Jubilee Path.

❷ **NX837549** Climb the single-track road, which swings right climbing past several houses. Beyond the last house, the road narrows down to a path. Follow this through open woodland for approximately 1 mile.

❸ **NX845542** Join a single-track road and pass the Barons Craig Hotel and some houses before the road swings right and drops down into Rockcliffe. Walk left along the pavement above the shore then turn right onto a single-track road signposted for 'The Merse and Castle Point'.

4 **NX850537** Follow the road past houses then take a path on the right, signposted Castle Point, along the rugged coastline. Cross a burn by a footbridge then fork right through scrubby woodland. Cross the top of a shingly beach and follow a path across another beach. At a coastal path signpost, go left up a narrow path past crags and the grave of Joseph Nelson (a crew member of The Ann which sank here in 1791). Beyond a gate, the path runs above the shore and climbs steadily. Go right into a field, along its edge and through a gate onto Castlehill Point.

5 **NX854524** Head left from the point, carefully following the cliff-edge and descending to a gate. Turn right along a field edge, passing one gate, then going through another. Climb a steep path onto the cliff top, though a gate and over the shoulder of Barcloy Hill, pausing for the stunning view back to Castlehill Point. At a drystane dyke the path bears right and descends seawards by some wooden steps. Beyond a gate, walk around rugged Gutcher's Isle, passing the remains of an old house.

6 **NX864527** Continue along the path, going through a gate and bearing right at a fork. A short detour right leads to a

monument to The Elbe, a schooner that sank in 1866. Continue along the field edge, and pass through three gates as the path rises steeply under White Hill. Then descend wooden steps into Portowarren.

7 **NX880535** Beyond a gate go left along a single-track road to Portling. Turn right, downhill, at a signpost for Sandyhills. Before reaching the shore, bear left up a flight of steps. Follow a path through three gates and climb steeply past Torrs Hill.

8 **NX887545** Descend steeply through a gate, go along a field-edge, through another gate and down three flights of steps. Fork left then left again and follow the path over a footbridge onto Sandyhills beach. Walk past a caravan site and leave the beach at the car park to reach the bus stop on the A710.

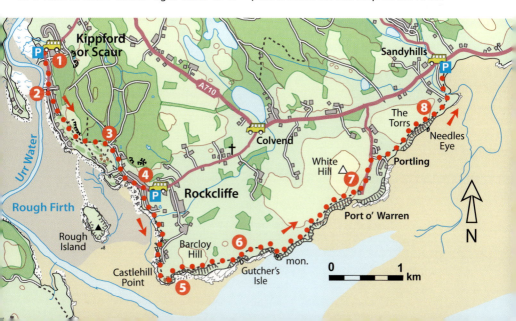

22

Enjoy the peace and seclusion of an intimate landscape of wooded peninsulas and sandy bays, lying at the heart of the East Stewartry Coast National Scenic Area.

Palnackie & Almorness Point

Start	Glen Road car park, Palnackie **NX823567**
Grade	☐☐☐☐☐
Distance	14km (8.75 miles)
Ascent	140m (460ft)
Time	4.5 hours
Terrain	Minor roads, woodland, coastal paths and tracks.

Getting there: Palnackie is on the A711, 3.5 miles south of Dalbeattie and 15 miles northeast of Kirkcudbright. Follow Glen Road past the post office and Riverside Drive then turn left to the car park.

Public transport: Regular ABC Travel Bus Service 505 from Dalbeattie and Kirkcudbright to Palnackie.

Palnackie is a quiet village with a population of about 150. It is on the River Urr, which flows from Loch Urr, 30 miles away, into Rough Firth. The village used to be a busy port, with 350-ton vessels being towed up the deep river channel from Kippford to Palnackie by horses. Today the river is noted for its salmon fishing.

White Port and Horse Isles Bay are two wonderful, secluded beaches near to Almorness Point. They are only accessible by boat or on foot, and so are incredibly peaceful and a haven for wildlife. Oystercatcher, curlew and heron feed on the shore and butterflies and dragonflies flit around the marshier ground. The views are spectacular particularly to Hestan Island, Rockcliffe, Castlehill Point and distant Southerness.

Orchardton Tower is near the route and is well worth a visit. It is an A-Listed building and the only circular tower house in Scotland, its inspiration possibly coming from Ireland where there are similar structures. The tower is 33 feet high and was built by John Cairns in the 15th century. It later passed through several hands, including the powerful Maxwell family, one of whom, Sir Robert Maxwell, fought at the Battle of Culloden in 1745.

BELOW: *The beautiful and secluded Horse Isles Bay (point 7)*

Most of the walk is on good paths and tracks, but between points **4** and **6** they can be very boggy and overgrown. Between **5** and **6**, the narrow way runs above a steep wooded slope.

1 **NX823567** Turn left from Glen Road car park into a single-track road, climbing steadily away from Palnackie with fine views over the meandering River Urr. The road descends beside Tornat Wood to South Glen Farm.

2 **NX827556** Keep straight ahead towards Glen Isle on a track that runs to the end of the wood then takes you to the shore of Rough Firth, where there is a delightful view across to Kippford (see the photograph on page 46).

3 **NX832552** Retrace your steps to South Glen Farm and turn left just before it.

4 **NX827556** Follow a track past the farm and through a gate. Go left, a short distance to second gate, left again and through a third gate. Then follow a track alongside mixed woodland. Continue through another gate and onto a path that can be very boggy in places, slowing progress.

5 **NX827546** Once through a further gate, bear right immediately onto a narrow path across a very boggy area. The path climbs gradually through woodland, rising above a steep slope where care should be taken. Exit the wood onto a wider track and pass a cottage. Follow the track down through a gate then across a field and through another gate to reach Almorness House.

6 **NX825536** Turn left, go through two gates onto a broad wooded track where red squirrels are regularly spotted. Stay on the main track for nearly 1.5 miles, eventually descending gently through heathland to secluded Horse Isles Bay, a beautiful spot with expansive views across Rough Firth.

7 **NX836523** A grassy track runs along the top of the beach then swings right to cross a footbridge. Immediately turn left across a short section of boggy ground before climbing over a small rise on a firmer path. Continue downhill to the secluded sandy beach at White Port.

8 **NX839518** Retrace your steps back to Almorness House (point **6**).

9 **NX825536** By Almorness House, turn left down its access drive, which quickly becomes a quiet, country road. Follow this through marvellous countryside for 1.5km (1 mile) to a junction (where Orchardton Tower is a short distance to the left). Continue straight on (northwards) for another mile to reach Palnackie, passing the Primary School as you return into the village. Follow the main street to a crossroads and turn right into Glen Road to return to the car park.

23

An invigorating clifftop walk leads from the charming village of the Isle of Whithorn, around the wild headland of Burrow Head, to St Ninian's Cave at secluded Port Castle Bay.

Isle of Whithorn & St Ninian

Start	Isle of Whithorn Harbour car park **NX478362**
Grade	☐☐☐☐☐
Distance	17.2km (10.75 miles)
Ascent	170m (550ft)
Time	4.5 to 6 hours
Terrain	Cliff paths, very exposed in places, stony beach and minor roads. Some steep ascents and descents.

Getting there: Isle of Whithorn is 21 miles south of Newton Stewart, via the A714 to Wigtown, the A7466 to Whithorn then the B7004. Follow Main Street through the village, turn right into Harbour Road then left at the end into the car park.
Public transport: Regular King of Kirkowan Bus Service 415 Newton Stewart to Isle of Whithorn.

BELOW: *Dramatic light illuminates the Isle of Whithorn at dusk (point 1)*

St Ninian's Chapel dates from around 1300, some 900 years after St Ninian established his mission, Candida Casa (The White House) at nearby Whithorn. For many centuries, the chapel was visited by pilgrims giving thanks for a safe arrival by sea before travelling on foot to St Ninian's shrine at Whithorn. A museum in Whithorn tells the story of the man believed to have introduced Christianity to Southern Scotland in around 390AD.

St Ninian's Cave is set into cliffs at the west end of Port Castle Bay. The saint is believed to have landed here or at the Isle of Whithorn at the start of his mission. A series of excavations from the late 1800s revealed several stone crosses and carvings dating from the 700s, thought to be the work of pilgrims and monks from Whithorn.

Burrow Head is the southern tip of the sparsely populated Machars. Dramatic cliffs, with many rock features, run along the indented coastline in both directions. They provide nesting sites for fulmar, shag, black guillemot, raven and peregrine. Inland lies well grazed maritime heath, where twite flit between patches of low scrub and great crested newts breed in small ponds.

As the name suggests, the Isle of Whithorn used to be an island. Improvements to the harbour, around 1790, included building a causeway to link it with the mainland and the village subsequently spread onshore. The paths along the cliffs, particularly around Burrow Head, are very exposed and extra care should be taken, especially in strong winds.

1 NX478362 From the car park follow a path away from the village to St Ninian's Chapel. The path extends to an old fort on the tip of the headland, where there are superb views. Return to the car park and walk around the harbour, past several houses then turn left onto Main Street. Walk past colourfully painted houses to a signposted path on the left, immediately after the Post Office. Follow it past a stone building and through a gate into a field. Take a path along the shore, going through further gates.

2 NX475361 Cross a footbridge and go through several gates, keeping to the field edge and hugging the coastline. Climb to a wall then go left where the path divides, continuing onto the clifftop. The path goes through a series of gates and is very exposed in places. The coast is spectacular with great pillars of rock rising from the sea. At Burrow Head, pass an old Coastguard station, swing right past a cairn then gradually descend.

3 NX452342 At Burrowhead Caravan Site, go through a gate and walk straight ahead past a few caravans. Go left along a tarmac road, which steadily climbs through the caravan site, then turn left onto a track and follow it down to a gate.

4 NX447343 Continue on a good path that undulates along the clifftop for 2 miles (3km), passing through a few more gates. There are spectacular views of the Mull of Galloway and the Isle of Man. Near Port Castle Bay, the path descends through one final gate. Bear right to join another path, which drops steeply down onto the shore. Walk across the stony beach to St Ninian's Cave, at the far end.

5 NX421360 Retrace your steps via the cliff path to the Caravan Park. On a clear day, the views extend as far as the Lake District.

6 NX447343 Follow the main road through the middle of the caravan site, passing a swimming pool, bar and shop. The road meanders through the site to the reception office and out onto a quiet single-track road.

7 NX452350 Pass several houses at Cutcloy and continue through attractive countryside. On the outskirts of the Isle of Whithorn, the lane descends into Tonderghie Road. At the T-junction with Main Street, turn right and walk back through the village to the harbour.

24

Rising nearly 2000 feet above the flat plains of the Solway Firth, Criffel dominates the surrounding landscape, with its conspicuous, whaleback shape visible from miles around.

Criffel & Knockendoch

Start	Sweetheart Abbey Car Park, New Abbey **NX965663**
Grade	☐☐☐☐☐
Distance	12km (7.5 miles)
Ascent	590m (1930ft)
Time	5 hours
Terrain	Forest tracks, hill paths, very boggy in places, and quiet country road. Steep ascents and descents.

Getting there: New Abbey is on the A710, 6 miles south of Dumfries
Public transport: Regular DGC Bus Service 372 Dumfries to New Abbey.

ABOVE: *The Nith Estuary from Knockendoch's summit (point 5)*

Criffel (569m) was named Kraka-fjell (Norse for Raven's Hill) by the Vikings. It is the most prominent landmark along the coast, commanding views to England and, on very clear days, the Isle of Man and Ireland. The six-foot Douglas Cairn marks the summit and legend is that one of the Earls of Morton is buried underneath it.

Loch Kindar is a beautiful small loch at the base of Criffel. It has two little islands, the largest of which is a crannog (a type of ancient island structure, found predominantly across Scotland and Ireland, used for loch-dwelling). Records from the 18th century tell of a large frame of oaks being visible and in recent years divers have confirmed its existence.

Much of the route can be very boggy and, in snow or poor weather, sound navigational skills are required. Good walking shoes/boots and appropriate clothing for the mountains are recommended.

❶ **NX965663** From the car park walk past Sweetheart Abbey and turn right onto Main Street (A710). Walk along the narrow pavement to The Square. Turn left before reaching the Cornmill. Follow a road towards the millpond and turn left before it onto a minor road, which is signposted for the Waterloo Monument.

❷ **NX962662** Follow this quiet, narrow road as it climbs gradually away from New Abbey, swinging sharply left then right before continuing to the foot of the wooded hills.

3 **NX957654** Go over a bridge onto a track, signposted for Criffel, taking the right fork at a cottage. Continue to the next cottage and here bear right onto a narrow, wooded path. Meet a track and turn right along it, climbing gradually. Follow it as it bends left then, where it bends sharply right, continue straight ahead onto a path through woodland. The path swings right into a firebreak between the conifers, where it becomes very boggy and climbs steeply, alongside a wall, up the lower slopes of Knockendoch.

4 **NX956642** Once above the treeline, follow the muddy path beside the wall to a fence where the wall swings away left. Go through a gap in the fence and climb the steep path south through heathery slopes, with great views opening out over the Nith Estuary and to the Moffat Hills. The path zigzags steeply up Knockendoch to its summit cairn.

5 **NX955632** The path bears southwest away from the cairn then crosses a boggy plateau. Follow it south then southeast, climbing more steeply as the upper slopes are reached. The path can be indistinct so take care here, especially in misty conditions. At the top, step over a low ruined wall to the Douglas Cairn, just east of Criffel's summit trig point. The views over the Solway coast and across the Nith estuary are marvellous.

6 **NX957619** Retrace your steps a short distance then bear right onto an indistinct path and descend northeast over more wet ground to Craigrockall Burn. Descend the path alongside the burn into woodland, where a firm path is picked up, and descend to a crossroads.

7 **NX964632** Go straight over and down the path to a broad track signposted for New Abbey. Turn left along it, bearing left at a junction. At a second junction, turn right down a path, passing through two gates, to Loch Kindar. Walk along a field edge beside the loch shore.

8 **NX965648** At the foot of the loch, swing left along the field-edge beside a strip of woodland. Go through a gate and over a track then bear left to cross another field, walking beside a ditch. At the far corner, exit by another gate. A grassy track then leads through a gap in a wall and alongside woodland. Go through a gate and cross a field to a final gate. Turn right onto the outward track, crossing the footbridge. Follow the road back to New Abbey.

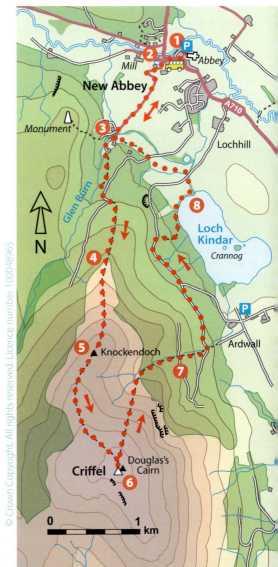

25

This imposing granite hill, one of the wildest places in southern Scotland, is home to red deer, peregrine falcon, red and black grouse and wild goats.

Cairnsmore of Fleet

Start	Car park near Muirfad **NX463631**
Grade	☐☐☐☐☐
Distance	19.2km (12 miles) or 12.8km (8 miles)
Ascent	1000m (3280ft) or 700m (2300ft)
Time	Main summit: 4 to 5 hours; whole route: 6 to 7 hours
Terrain	Good hill paths, but pathless terrain on the summits. Sustained ascent and descent.

Getting there: The start is 4 miles southeast of Newton Stewart and 3.5 miles north of Creetown. Turn off the A75 into Muirfad and bend left. Bear left where the single-track road forks then go first right into the car park.
Public transport: Regular Stagecoach Bus Service 500 from Stranraer or Dumfries to Muirfad.

Cairnsmore of Fleet (711m/2333ft) is the highest point along the Galloway Coast and a stunning vantage point, providing a window into the remoter upland areas of Galloway. The Merrick (Galloway's highest mountain), the Mull of Galloway, Wigtown Bay, the Isle of Man, Ailsa Craig, Ayrshire and Kintyre are visible from the exposed summit plateau. By continuing to Meikle Multaggart and the Knee of Cairnsmore, you can experience a real sense of the wildness of this part of Galloway.

Cairnsmore of Fleet National Nature Reserve supports a distinctive range of flora because of its granite bedrock and high rainfall. The wind-swept summit heath has a short carpet of dwarf willow, stiff sedge and woolly fringe moss; the heather moorland lower down contains bell heather, cotton grass and blaeberry, while sphagnum moss, hair moss and common butterwort thrive on the blanket bog.

BELOW: *Returning to Cairnsmore of Fleet from Meikle Mulltaggart (point 7)*

Although the walk is mainly on good paths, the summit plateau is largely pathless, so in snow or poor weather you need good navigation skills. Sound walking shoes/boots and appropriate clothing for the mountains is recommended.

❶ NX463631 Walk across the car park and go through a gate. Turn left onto a single-track road and follow it, climbing gradually and crossing a burn by an old stone bridge.

Keep right at a fork to pass the walled garden of Cairnsmore House. Just before Cairnsmore Farm, turn right onto a signposted path.

② **NX470638** Follow the path as it meanders through woodland to a narrow road. Turn left and walk past the farm, keeping straight ahead on a track. Go through a gate and bear right, diagonally uphill across a field (where livestock may be grazing).

③ **NX474643** Go through a gate and follow a fine path through oak and sycamore woodland. Cross a stile then climb steeply through a replanted area with saplings. Once through a gap in a wall, the path enters a conifer forest and continues steeply upwards.

④ **NX479648** Cross a track and keep climbing through the trees along a forest ride, which can be boggy in places. Eventually, you rise out of the forest onto the heather clad lower slopes of Cairnsmore of Fleet, where great views along Wigtown Bay to the Mull of Galloway await.

⑤ **NX492654** Continue over a stile then climb steeply, via zigzags, onto the flat summit plateau. Here the path bears left to continue north (past a monument commemorating several plane crashes) to the trig point and cairn at the top of Cairnsmore of Fleet, where there is a wonderful 360-degree panorama.

⑥ **NX502671** You can retrace the path from here back to the car park. For the full route, pass the trig point and walk northeast across

pathless terrain, then descend steep, grassy slopes to a col. Pick up a path, which rises steeply onto the rounded summit of Meikle Multaggert. This spot has expansive and lonely views that emphasise the wildness of the region and its central position amongst the Galloway Hills.

⑦ **NX512678** Retrace your steps onto Cairnsmore, but just before the trig point bear left and cross the featureless plateau (which provides good walking), heading southwards. Follow the plateau edge around the steep, craggy face of the fantastically named Spout of the Clinks and join an indistinct path beside an old fence. Follow this steeply down to a col then climb up onto the Knee of Cairnsmore. Walk along the top to the cairn at the south end.

⑧ **NX509654** Retrace your steps back towards the main summit and, once on the plateau, bear left to pick up the outward path. Follow it back down to the start.

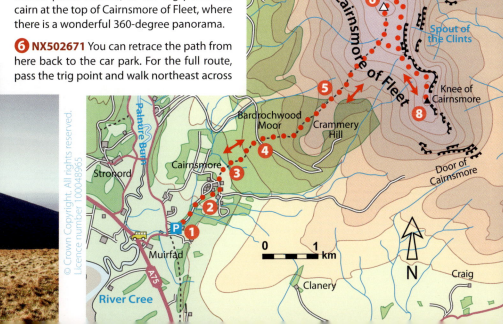

Enjoying the Outdoors

Dumfries and Galloway Council have a duty to uphold public access rights and you should contact their access officers if you find any route obstructed. The council employs countryside rangers, who help people to enjoy the outdoors responsibly and who organise events such as guided wildlife walks.

Several other organisations also promote access on their land, often with waymarked paths, and some employ rangers to work with the public.

The Scottish Outdoor Access Code describes how to enjoy the outdoors responsibly.

Dumfries and Galloway Council
Planning and the Environment
Tel. 030 33 33 3000
www.dumgal.gov.uk

Scottish Natural Heritage
Tel. 01387 247010
www.snh.gov.uk

Forestry Commission Scotland
Dumfries and Borders Forest District
Tel. 01387 860247
Galloway Forest District
Tel. 01671 402420
www.forestry.gov.uk

RSPB Southwest Scotland
Tel. 0141 331 0993
www.rspb.org.uk

Scottish Wildlife Trust
Tel. 0131 312 7765
www.scottishwildlifetrust.org.uk

Wildfowl & Wetlands Trust (WWT)
WWT Caerlaverock Wetland Centre
Tel. 01387 770200
www.wwt.org.uk

Dumfries and Galloway Environmental Resources Centre provides wildlife and habitat information: www.dgerc.org.uk

Enjoy Scotland's outdoors responsibly

Everyone has the right to be on most land and inland water providing they act responsibly. Your access rights and responsibilities are explained fully in the Scottish Outdoor Access Code.

Whether you're in the outdoors or managing the outdoors, the key things are to:

- **take responsibility for your own actions**
- **respect the interests of other people**
- **care for the environment.**

Visit **outdooraccess-scotland.com** or contact your local Scottish Natural Heritage office.

Travel & tourist information

Getting to Galloway

Rail

Scotrail provides excellent rail links to Dumfries from Glasgow, Newcastle and Carlisle, and from Glasgow to Stranraer: tel. 0845 601 5929, www.scotrail.co.uk.

Bus

Scottish Citylink runs direct services from Glasgow to Stranraer and Dumfries, and also from Edinburgh to Stranraer: tel. 0871 266 33 33, www.citylink.co.uk.

Stagecoach runs direct services between Carlisle and Dumfries: tel. 01387 253496, www.stagecoachbus.com.

MacEwan's Coaches run direct services from Edinburgh to Dumfries: tel: 01387 711 123.

Sea

P&O Ferries sail from Larne to Cairnryan or Troon: tel. 08716 642121, www.poferries.com. **StenaLine** sail from Belfast to Cairnryan: tel. 08447 70 70 70, www.stenaline.co.uk.

Getting around by bus

Several providers run regular services to all corners of Galloway.

Stagecoach West Scotland: tel. 01387 253496, www.stagecoachbus.com.

ABC Travel: tel. 01671 830284.

DGC Buses: tel. 01387 260383.

King of Kirkowan: tel. 01671 830284.

For more journey planning information ring **Traveline Scotland** on 0871 200 22 33 or visit www.travelinescotland.com.

Accommodation

Dumfries & Galloway Tourist Office can provide more information on Galloway's superb hotels, B&Bs, self-catering cottages and campsites: tel. 01387 253862, www.visitdumfriesandgalloway.co.uk.

Visitor Information Centres

Gretna: Gretna Gateway Outlet Village, Gretna, DG16 5GG, tel. 01461 337834.
Dumfries: 64 White Sands, Dumfries, DG1 2RS, tel. 01387 253 862.
Castle Douglas: Market Hill Car Park, Castle Douglas, DG7 1AE, tel. 01556 502611.
Kirkcudbright: Harbour Square, Kirkcudbright, DG6 4HY, tel. 01557 330494.
Gatehouse of Fleet: Mill on the Fleet, High Street, Gatehouse of Fleet, DG7 2HS, tel. 01557 814212.
Newton Stewart: Dashwood Square, Newton Stewart, DG10 9JU, tel. 01671 402431.
Stranraer: 28 Harbour Street, Stranraer, DG9 7RA, tel. 01776 702595.

ABOVE: *Old boat by the River Dee in Kirkcudbright (walk 3)*
OPPOSITE: *Enjoying the view over the Colvend Coast (walk 21)*

About this guidebook

Author

Outdoors writer and photographer Keith Fergus has walked all over Scotland but the Galloway Coast remains a particular favourite. Over many years visiting the region Keith has built up an intimate knowledge of the coastline, its incredible history, exceptional wildlife and breath-taking scenery.

As well as writing for a variety of outdoor magazines, Keith runs his own photographic business and photo library, which – under the banner of *Scottish Horizons* – produces a wide range of postcards, greetings cards and calendars: **www.scottishhorizons.co.uk**. Keith lives with his wife and two children on the outskirts of Glasgow. This is his fourth book.

Publisher

Catkin Press is a is a small, independent publisher based in Scotland. Our books aim to help readers enjoy healthy, active lives that are in touch with nature.

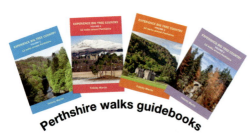

Perthshire walks guidebooks

The first titles on Catkin Press's list were four volumes of *Experience Big Tree Country: 12 Walks around Perthshire*. The set of guidebooks describe 48 of the best walks in Perthshire and highlight the natural history of the area. They are available widely and at a discount via the Catkin Press website.

About this guidebook

Please contact Catkin Press if you find inaccuracies in either the text or the maps when walking these routes. While every care has been taken to ensure the accuracy of route directions, the publishers cannot accept responsibility for errors or omissions, or changes in details given. Updates will be available on the Catkin Press website.

The paper this guide is printed on is 9 Lives 80 Silk containing 80% recovered fibre and 20% virgin fibre sourced from sustainable forests.

You can help the environment, reduce your carbon footprint and support local services by using public transport.

Catkin Press
Ellangowan, Polinard, Comrie,
Perthshire PH6 2HJ
info@catkinpress.com
www.catkinpress.com